Instructing for Results

Instructing for Results

Fredric H. Margolis
Chip R. Bell

University Associates, Inc.
San Diego, California

&

Lakewood Publications
Minneapolis, Minnesota

Copyright © 1986 by University Associates, Inc.
ISBN: 0-88390-196-X
Library of Congress Catalog Card Number 86-50409
Printed in the United States of America

Acknowledgments

Taking a book from idea to publication is an interdependent effort. We have many to thank for their energies on our behalf.

Malcolm Knowles provided more than the conceptual foundation for the book. As the "Father of Adult Learning," Malcolm has had a profound influence on our work with the people who train adults. We have been inspired for years by his personal encouragement and his professional congruence. We hope that this book contributes to his lifetime legacy of helping adults to learn.

Margaret Ladd, Leslie Stephen, and Larry Nolan Davis provided useful assistance on the early drafts of the book. Nancy Bell gave valuable encouragement and support throughout.

Finally, we wish to thank the many client organizations and workshop participants who gave us the opportunity to test and refine the ideas and techniques in the book.

Fredric H. Margolis
Chip R. Bell

Foreword

This is one of the most clearly and interestingly written, theoretically sound, and practically useful books on how to produce effective learning experiences in human resource development that I have seen. It is not a how-to-do-it book in the sense of prescribing a lock-step set of procedures for delivering a standardized program. Rather, it describes a procedural process that is rich in options for tailoring a program that will be geared to the unique circumstances of various situations and the unique characteristics of various individual participants.

I am certain that this book will give newcomers in training and adult-education roles the necessary guidelines to begin performing with confidence. But I have been in the business for almost fifty years, and I found myself feeling reinforced, inspired, and stimulated with new ideas from my reading of the book. So it is useful for veterans, as well. It is a valuable addition to our literature.

Malcolm S. Knowles
Professor Emeritus, North Carolina State University

This is the book that has been sought for a long time by those who have responsibility for delivering learning experiences. The authors, from their vast experience, have given us insight into how to set the learning climate and how to deliver learning. It will be helpful for the experienced deliverer, as well as for those with little or no experience. Each will find something of value in this book.

Leonard Nadler
Professor, The George Washington University

Guidelines on how to help people learn seem unnecessary to many who feel that the acquisition of new knowledge, skills, and attitudes is dependent entirely on the learner's motivation. In reality, however, we need to be professionally competent when serving as trainers, coaches, developers, or teachers in order to help make the learning process as potentially useful as possible.

Those of us who act as learning facilitators should know ourselves well enough that we *help* rather than hinder the learning. To be at our best—and put the learning process in perspective so it is seen as enjoyable, frustrating, difficult, varied, challenging, and sometimes successful—is essential. If you take yourself too seriously and overplan, overdirect, and assume you have control of the learning, the chances that learning will take place become remote. This book has that perspective.

Remember that to facilitate learning with others, we must also be learners. The way this book looks at the facilitator's role helps us understand the fragile and complex nature of creating and implementing significant learning experiences. While we cannot control the occurrence of a learning experience, we can influence it as well as increase the chance of its occurring more frequently. Stimulating the learner readiness to "surface," to come into consciousness, and to be confronted can be encouraged. As indicated in *Instructing for Results*, this requires us to become innovative and professional in orchestrating "designs for learning" that create optimum stimulus, excitement, and insight potential that will increase the chances that a learning experience will occur.

The Late Gordon L. Lippitt
Professor, The George Washington University
President, American Society for Training and Development
President, Organization Renewal, Inc.

Preface

The trainer stands alone in front of a group. Although this situation may evoke some anxiety, the experienced trainer—who knows what to do and how to do it—is also likely to feel confident.

The experience that gives rise to the confidence comes only after many successes and some failures. In the field of training, successes cannot be guaranteed and failures cannot be avoided. However, trainers can do some things that greatly increase the probability of success: They can be prepared, know the content or subject matter of the training, be motivated to help people to learn, and have a good understanding of the process of delivering training.

This book is about the *process* of instructing for results. It describes a number of training delivery techniques that work. Some of them we discovered by trial and error combined with reflection and revision; others are based on theories developed by our predecessors and colleagues in the profession; still others are outgrowths of our own theories.

Most of those who deliver training have not prepared themselves academically for the job. Instead, they have found themselves in the role more or less by accident. Often people are "drafted" into the job of training because they have become knowledgeable about particular subjects or proficient in particular skills. Sometimes people are selected to be trainers because they can express thoughts clearly and can appear comfortable when speaking to groups. On some occasions people are assigned the responsibility of training because of their enthusiasm or their warm personalities. On still other occasions people are asked to assume the role of trainer as a necessary step in their career paths. Finally, some people find themselves in front of groups simply because they were the only ones available who were willing to do the job.

Regardless of the circumstances that led you to the job, if you have stayed in it for more than a session or two, it is probably because you like training and are doing it reasonably well. The concepts and suggestions in this book are offered as a resource for you to use in refining and improving the strengths that you have already begun demonstrating.

Fredric H. Margolis
Bethesda, Maryland

Chip R. Bell
Charlotte, North Carolina

May, 1986

Contents

Introduction

DELIVERING TRAINING

The word *deliver* can connote several different meanings. It can mean such pleasant things as setting something free, aiding in the birth process, and helping to produce expected results. In addition, it can refer to such actions as giving something to another person or uttering the lines of a speech. Although the last two meanings are probably most commonly associated with the word *deliver* in the context of training, a trainer does, in fact, set free, aid in the birth process, and help to produce expected results. When trainers appear before groups of people assembled for a training session, their goal is to *deliver* knowledge in the most positive sense of that word.

The word *training*, as used in this book, means *helping adults to learn.* This function involves more than "serving up" information; it involves instructing *for results* so that people can learn how to digest and use the information that is provided. The *trainer* can be a manager, an executive, an educator, a consultant, a group facilitator, or any other person who is responsible for assisting in learning. Although this book is intended as a basic text and was written with the needs of the new trainer particularly in mind, it is hoped that even seasoned trainers will find new ideas or insights. Experienced trainers may discover that some of the techniques and practices we suggest seem preferable to what they have been doing—even when what they have been doing works. Regardless of your level of experience, we encourage you to adapt our ideas freely and to modify them as necessary in an effort to develop and/or increase delivery skills.

WHAT, HOW TO, AND WHY

This is more than a "how-to" book. "How-to" books suggest *what* to do and *when* to do it. We believe that without a *why*, a description of *how to* is an empty formula. Consequently, this book offers proven techniques that help adults to learn and explains why these techniques work. It also deals with certain techniques that have proven unsuccessful and explains why this is the case.

Training involves two distinctly different kinds of activities—*designing* and *delivering*. Sometimes the same person does both, but often the person who designs does not deliver, and the person who delivers did not design. A good design can be butchered by inept delivery, and great delivery skills cannot rescue a poor design. Both must work in concert to produce an effective training program.

In writing a book about delivery, such as this one, it would be irresponsible not to include a few suggestions about dealing with poor designs; therefore, some material about designing is included in this book. In addition, numerous related tasks must be performed well in order for a training program to achieve its potential, and several of these activities are discussed.

Ultimately, anyone who writes a book about training must draw the line somewhere regarding what to include. The following material clarifies how and where we drew the line with regard to this book's content.

Delivery. This subject constitutes the main focus of the book.

Managing Yourself. The notion of managing yourself as a trainer encompasses such concerns as preparing for a training session, handling anxiety and nervousness, and dealing with feelings of success or failure. A number of suggestions are included throughout this book when such concerns are relevant.

Conference Management. Conference management refers to the function of arranging for and monitoring the use of such things as meeting rooms, furniture, equipment, audiovisual aids, and refreshments. Chapter 2, "Making Arrangements," provides many suggestions for handling the logistics of a training program. In addition, a number of tips are presented in other chapters when they are relevant to the effectiveness of a training program.

Evaluation. In this book, evaluation is dealt with in terms of program delivery and how you can interpret evaluative feedback and use it to improve.

Training Design. A detailed discussion of design issues is beyond the scope of this book; if you are interested in pursuing this subject, refer to the Resources appendix. In various places throughout the book, however, your attention is drawn to design matters that govern the delivery of a program—for example, the extent to which a program's delivery relies on the use of particular materials and equipment.

The practices suggested in this book are not applicable to all types of training, but they are applicable to many of the most common types offered in today's organizations. For example, these practices apply to all management and supervisory training, regardless of the type of organization involved or its mission. They also apply to all cognitive, analytic, and interpersonal skills-training programs—for salespeople, for example, or for technical and professional staff. But they may be less useful for programs devoted to technical-skills training, such as how to operate a forklift or perform a specific task on an assembly line.

In addition, we opted to focus on delivering training to relatively small groups of learners. Although the principles and techniques described can work with groups of any size, trainers often find that they are most effective with groups of twelve to twenty-five.

HOW TO USE THIS BOOK

It is recommended that you proceed to Chapter 1 next because it provides a basis for all the remaining chapters. Subsequent chapters are organized more or less sequentially, considering in turn each activity that you would normally undertake in instructing. Consequently, if you are a beginning trainer you may find it useful to read the chapters in sequence as they are presented.

If you are a more-experienced trainer you may find it preferable to read the chapters in a different order that seems more appropriate as preparation for a particular session. One approach is to begin with

Chapter 5, "Giving Instructions," since this subject is one that must be dealt with in almost all training sessions. It is also useful to review selected chapters after a session; this approach can help in forming a clear picture of what worked well and what needs improvement.

Chapter 1

What Training Involves

In describing training, it is important to specify not only *what* it is—
the tasks commonly associated with it—but also *how* it is done—
your style or approach to completing the necessary tasks. In this
chapter both subjects are explored. Because your training style colors
everything that you do, it is addressed first.

THE TRAINER'S STYLE

A person who is responsible for delivering training generally adopts
a "training style" that has been used by someone else. Sometimes a
particular style is emulated because the trainer admires it. Occasionally,
the style adopted is a result of the trainer's recognizing "the way things
are done around here." On still other occasions, a style is chosen
because it represents the only way in which the trainer has seen things
done; the trainer assumes—not always correctly—that it is the "right"
way.

   Our viewpoint is that style, as it refers to *presentation technique,* is not critical: Almost anything you do is acceptable as long
as it helps people to learn (or at least does not hinder their learning).
But style also refers to *assumptions and beliefs* about how adults learn
and what is done to facilitate that learning. These assumptions and
beliefs may relate to the issues of authority, control, and obedience,
or they may concern an assessment of the intelligence or motivation
of particular groups of learners. Whatever their content, they affect
not only the way in which you train but also *how* learners learn. Consequently, it is important that you develop an awareness of your
assumptions and beliefs.

Style Stereotypes

The following descriptions of stereotyped training styles are intended to stimulate your thinking about your style. The underlying assumption of each style is indicated with quotation marks. Although these assumptions are exaggerated, they reveal the implications of the styles involved and may help you to become more aware of the "hidden whys" behind any style (or combination of styles) that you have adopted or admired.

The Professor. "The students should take good notes because what I say is important and they learn by paying attention to me. Later I'll test them on this material so that I can confirm what they have learned." The professorial style implies that the trainer's approval, not the learners' subsequent performance, is the goal of learning.

The Comedian. "I'll keep the learners laughing, and they'll go away feeling good." The comedian confuses entertainment with training.

The Projectionist. "This film will tell the learners what they need to know. If the projector works, it'll be a good session." The projectionist tends to rely on things like audiovisual aids to accomplish the training. This approach de-emphasizes the trainer's obligation to help others to learn.

The Inspirer. "I'll pump them up and then send them out to do it." The trainer who adopts the inspirational style confuses excitement, which often dissipates quickly, with motivation. Adult learning and performance depend on the learners' understanding and acceptance of the rationale behind the training experience.

The Drill Instructor. "I'll tell them what I'm going to tell them; then I'll tell them; then I'll tell them what I told them." The military drill-instructor style assumes that learners are dense or do not want to learn in the first place. Such an assumption is often self-fulfilling.

It is the negative assumption behind each of these exaggerated style descriptions, rather than the trainer's behavior in and of itself, that may affect the learners in a negative way and impede their learning. For this reason you need to assess and continually monitor your style in terms of its actual or potential impact on learners.

Assumptions

Assumptions about training and beliefs about how adults learn often come from personal experience—in a college lecture hall or a job-training program—or from studying the classic learning theories. However, we believe that adult learning is a vastly more complex phenomenon than some of the classic theories suggest.

Our assumptions and the practices we suggest in the remainder of this book center around the concept of andragogy. The term *andragogy* refers to a point of view about adult learning that asserts that the learners themselves assume a primary role in organizing and using new information and skills. Malcolm S. Knowles, a leading educational theorist and adult educator, coined the term and formulated the philosophy behind it.

Knowles identified five assumptions[1] about adult learners that we believe are fundamental to effective delivery:

1. Adults are motivated to learn as they develop needs and interests that learning will satisfy. Therefore, learners' needs and interests are the appropriate starting points for organizing adult-learning activities, and they are the crucial guideposts for delivering training.

2. Adult orientation to learning is centered around life or work. Therefore, the appropriate frameworks for organizing adult learning are life- and/or work-related situations, not academic or theoretical subjects.

3. Experience is the richest resource for adult learning. Therefore, the core methodology for adult-learning programs involves actively participating in a planned series of experiences, analyzing those experiences, and determining their application to work and life situations.

---

[1]Adapted from: (1)*The Modern Practice of Adult Education: From Pedagogy to Andragogy* by M. Knowles. Copyright 1980 by Cambridge Book Company, 888 Seventh Avenue, New York, NY 10106. Adapted with the permission of the publisher. (2)*The Adult Learner: A Neglected Species* (3rd ed.) by M. Knowles, published in 1984 by Gulf, Houston, Texas. Adapted with the permission of the publisher.

4. Adults have a deep need to be self-directing. Therefore, the role of the trainer is to engage in a process of inquiry, analysis, and decision making with learners rather than to transmit his or her knowledge to them and then evaluate their conformity to it.

5. Individual differences among adult learners increase with age and experience. Therefore, adult-learning programs must make optimum provision for differences in style, time, place, and pace of learning.

Perhaps the most important conclusion to be drawn from these assumptions is that the adult learner is in charge of his or her own learning. This notion forms the basis for andragogy. You can *assist* learners in acquiring new knowledge and developing new skills, but you cannot do the learning for them.

TRAINING VERSUS TEACHING

We believe that to translate the assumptions of andragogy into action, it is important for you to think of yourself as a *trainer* rather than a *teacher*.

Figure 1-1 presents some of the differences between teaching and training. The basic difference is this: A teacher traditionally controls the process and the content of learning by defining the situation and the procedures and by specifying what is right and what is wrong. Teaching environments may include foreign-language classes, programmed-instruction classes, driver-training school, and a fifth-grade classroom.

Training environments, on the other hand, are those in which the trainer defines the process through which learning takes place. The trainer guides the learners in determining the relevance of the learning for their own lives and work; the learners are encouraged to use their own judgment and decision-making capabilities. Training environments may include management-skills seminars or planning workshops sponsored by organizations.

	Teaching	Training
Underlying Philosophy	• Knowledge is passed from the teacher to the learner.	• Knowledge is discovered through mutual investigation of problems and issues.
	• Organizations are improved through technical advances.	• Organizations are improved by developing the resources and allowing learners to direct their own capabilities.
	• Instruction is teacher oriented.	• Instruction is learner oriented.
Assessment of Needs for and Results of Instruction	• Observable, measurable behavior is examined.	• Attitudes as well as behavior are examined.
Learning Objectives	• Measurable and precise behavioral objectives are required. • The acquisition of information is emphasized.	• Degree of precision in objectives is tailored to what is being learned. • Interpersonal and self-directing competencies are emphasized.
Content	• Technical knowledge and skills, psychomotor skills, languages, mathematics, and science are appropriate content for teaching.	• Interpersonal and other kinds of skills requiring some degree of analysis and judgment, managerial skills, and the arts and humanities are appropriate content for training.
Learning Methods	• The structure of the content is oriented toward the subject; the the process of devising instructional methods tends to be mechanical.	• The structure of the content is oriented toward the learners and the situation.
	• Programmed learning, lecture, and audiovisual methods are primarily used.	• Discovery learning methods are used.
	• Delivery is based on presentation and participative methods that are designed to produce the prescribed, measurable result.	• Delivery is based on presentation and participative methods that are designed to enhance skills of analysis, judgment, and problem solving.

Figure 1-1. Teaching Versus Training

Trainer Characteristics

You are a leader, not a dictator, a traffic officer, or a three-star general. You have the responsibility for making decisions regarding the content of the training experience, for providing guidance, and for serving as a resource for the learners. Although you may be an authority on a particular subject matter, it is still up to the learners to determine how, when, or, in some cases, *if* the ideas presented in a session should be integrated into their work or personal lives. This does not mean that training is a passive, "laid-back," "go-with-the-flow" process. On the contrary, you are a facilitator, the catalyst for learning; you make it possible for learning to happen by guiding learners through the activities that the training design requires.

There are five basic activities involved in delivering training:

1. Setting and maintaining a learning climate;
2. Making presentations;
3. Giving instructions;
4. Monitoring group and individual tasks; and
5. Managing the reporting process.

Each of these activities is described in detail in the following chapters.

One of your major responsibilities is directing the process through which learning occurs. This is very different from controlling the content of the session or controlling the learners. You are not the ultimate repository of wisdom; you know a lot of useful information that can be shared, but so do the learners. Your objective is to sensitively guide the process whereby learners exchange information and learn from the activities designed into the session.

Confidence and Competence

It is extremely important that you project confidence and competence. In order to engage in useful work in the training environment, learners must sense you know what you are doing. Obviously, that acceptance makes things a lot more pleasant for you, too.

For this reason, it is necessary for you to become intimately familiar with the content and process of the training program to be delivered.

You must ensure that the design demonstrates emotional logic as well as content logic; both must be present in any training session to foster maximum learning and maximum application of learning. Work to understand how every component of the design contributes to achieving the training goals. Once these prerequisites have been met, you will feel competent and confident to begin the session.

Be aware of the learners' needs and learning processes as well as what they are learning. Be prepared to make adjustments as needed in the amount of time that the different parts of the program might require. If it seems appropriate to say more in a presentation than what has been provided in pre-existing content, follow this instinct.

The saying that "God's time is not the same as trainer's time" refers to the practice of stretching time limits for group work, depending on how the learning is proceeding. Specific times for each experience are indicated in most training designs, but these are guidelines rather than requirements. You are responsible for allocating sufficient time for each learning activity, but you also have the responsibility for being flexible rather than rigid in doing this. When learners are involved in an exercise, it is essential that you are aware of how long it takes them to do the task. It is rarely a good idea to decrease the time, but occasionally it is necessary to allow more time.

As you gain experience with a training program, you will develop ways to make it uniquely suited to the organization's needs as well as to your personal style. It is usually important to learn and follow whatever pre-existing design there might be because it has been carefully structured to promote learning. It is not necessary, however, to follow that design rigidly or slavishly.

Authenticity

It is extremely important for you to be authentic—that is, to be yourself. A training session is not the time to decide to "perform" in the style of your boss, spouse, therapist, or best friend. The problem with trying to assume someone else's style of behavior—really a form of acting—is that it does little to help people to learn. Trainers who act make themselves the center of attention. Learning occurs best when adults feel comfortable and act naturally; so relax and be yourself.

It is equally important to be sincere. When you make a supportive statement to someone, really *feel* it. For example, avoid saying things like "that's good" when you don't mean it; insincerity will show in your voice and body; such comments also may sound patronizing. The old maxim "Say what you mean and mean what you say" is worth remembering when delivering training.

Being authentic and "professional" at the same time may seem difficult at first. If you have a very soft voice, you will have to project it consciously so that learners can hear what is being said. Work to control any nervous mannerisms, and censor language that might be offensive to someone. With practice, it is possible to find an appropriate blend of authenticity and professionalism. This book is full of tips and techniques that will be helpful in this respect.

One more thing: Enjoy the experience of delivering training. Stop to savor the moment when you and the learners experience a sense of joy or satisfaction with an accomplishment. The more satisfying the session is for you, the more satisfying it will be for the learners.

Chapter 2

Making Arrangements

Planning and preparation are the keys to program success. Inexperienced trainers find that thorough preparation helps to allay many fears and increase confidence. Experienced trainers know that attention to detail helps programs to run smoothly and professionally.

Great professional golfers generally walk the course before a tournament, mentally playing each shot perfectly. That visualization provides both a practice run and an ideal model to follow. You can derive much the same benefit by mentally rehearsing how to deliver the program and by using a check list for preparation and planning.

SELECTING A SITE

Basic Requirements

Every training site creates its own special environment, atmosphere, or mood. A rustic retreat projects a different ambience than does the board room on the 99th floor of a corporation's headquarters. Any site—whether it is classroom B, the Acorn Suite at the Holiday Inn, or the division conference room—can be perfectly adequate or totally inappropriate, depending on the purpose of the training, the expectations of the trainer, and the requirements of the training. Most sites can be altered to be satisfactory.

A good training site meets the following basic requirements:

Comfort and accessibility. If the site is austere or primitive, learners may spend their energy worrying about their discomfort. If the site is remote, learners may arrive exhausted, or they may have difficulty in finding it.

Quiet, privacy, and freedom from interruptions. External noise or interruptions, such as phone calls for learners, will drain your momentum and break the learners' train of thought. It is also important to be aware of and to prepare for the possibility of such things as lawn mowers outside, loud typewriters next door, and intercoms.

Ample space. Space is a major consideration in site selection because cramped conditions inhibit program success. Insure that the site is sufficiently spacious to allow you to move easily among small groups and to allow visual aids to be seen clearly by all learners. Too large a room poses different problems: It is difficult to create an atmosphere of togetherness in excessive space, and the acoustics may be bad. Later in this chapter the subject of room setup will be addressed in greater detail.

Suitability for subgroup activity. Picture this situation: A major university asked one of the authors to conduct an all-day workshop featuring activities that require learners to form subgroups. The site selected by the sponsor was a gigantic lecture hall. The interior design was "early amphitheater"—hundreds of seats fanning out row after row from a small pit containing a large lectern and a small chalkboard. The chairs were bolted to the floor. Clearly, this arrangement was a study in how to discourage subgroup interaction.

In addition to the basic requirements just described, consider these conditions:

- Are restrooms available nearby?
- Are electrical outlets present in the room in areas where they are needed?
- Is the room properly ventilated?
- Can the room be comfortably heated or cooled? Can the temperature be controlled?
- Are the chairs comfortable?
- Is the light bright enough to prevent eye strain but soft enough to project warmth?

On-Site Versus Off-Site Programs

On-site programs are generally more economical, and they usually are easier to set up and manage. Familiarity also can aid learners in feeling comfortable and secure.

However, on-site locations also present drawbacks. Executives can easily drop in, potentially adding a note of anxiety. In addition, learners are more likely to be interrupted by phone calls. Although familiar surroundings contribute to a sense of security, they also make it more difficult for learners to separate themselves mentally from the pressures of their daily work. On the other hand, conducting a program in a conference room on "mahogany row" may produce more formality and evoke less candor than you desire.

Off-site locations give learners the opportunity to escape the constraints of the work place and to focus on the topic at hand. In addition, casual dress is possible in an off-site location. The change of environment also can enhance the growth that you are trying to foster.

Like on-site locations, off-site locations also present disadvantages. You will have to coordinate the training from a distance. It takes energy and time for learners to acclimate to the new environment. Finally, you may have less control over the surroundings. Some trainers tell stories of beginning a program in the Acorn Suite, only to be interrupted halfway through by the Apex Company sales rally in the suite next door, complete with raucous laughter and frequent applause.

SETTING THE TIME

The time selected for a training program should fit the norms and habits of the learners. If they are accustomed to coming to work at 9:00 a.m., starting the program at 8:00 a.m. may mean that latecomers will miss the opening. Scheduling the program to go over the normal lunch hour or past the time at which learners typically leave work could be self-defeating: Clock watching will draw attention away from the learning.

Sometimes scheduling the program to end thirty minutes to an hour before learners normally leave work assures them that they can return to their work stations after training to "touch base" with their operations. This can eliminate hasty office visits or mad dashes to the phone during breaks. Whether it involves morning, afternoon, or evening hours, the program schedule must accommodate the learners' work schedules.

NOTIFYING LEARNERS

Once learners have been identified, it is important that you help them to prepare mentally for the training program. If it is not possible to meet with each learner before the program, send an invitation memorandum or letter. The point is to let the learners know the purpose of the training program and to give them an overview of how it will be conducted. Apprise learners of the length of the program, the time to arrive, the location, the appropriate dress, and what they should bring. If they do not need to bring anything, state this in your communication. Encourage learners to contact you if they have any questions. Figure 2-1 presents a sample invitation memorandum.

Avoid explaining the details of the training design in the invitation memorandum. Such details may be misunderstood, causing unnecessary anxiety or diverting attention from the goals of the program. Learners simply need a sense of the subject matter of the program. You can answer specific questions during short meetings or telephone calls.

Sometimes learners want to know who else will be attending the program. If the training is to be conducted off site, sending a list of learners to each person invited can be helpful with regard to the learners' arranging transportation or requesting roommates if an overnight stay is involved. By sending a list of learners, you also may relieve someone's anxiety about being the only man (woman, black, young person, or whatever) in the group.

AVOIDING LEARNER RESISTANCE

Occasionally learners may be attending the program "against their will." For example, the program may be perceived as a figurative hoop through which people must jump to be promoted or to be certified

To: New Supervisors
From: Jimmie Steele
Subject: Selection-Interviewing Program
Date: March 21

You are cordially invited to attend a selection-interviewing training program to be conducted on Tuesday, April 18, from 8:30 a.m. to 12:00 noon in Conference Room 6. The program has been developed to provide you with an opportunity to practice your skills in conducting an effective selection interview.

This is an important and valuable program. If you are not able to attend, please let me know so that another person can be invited.

If you have any questions about your participation in this program, please call me at extension 336.

cc: S. Tipton
    P. Plott
    R. Morgan

Figure 2-1. Sample Invitation Memorandum

or qualified in some way. For whatever reason, mandatory attendance tends to translate into learner resistance to the program and to learning.

Learning programs are most effective when:

- They represent a response to an identified learning need that is directly related to work or life situations;
- They help learners to perform their current or future jobs more effectively; and
- The learner and his or her supervisor have discussed both the reason for attendance and their respective expectations following completion of the program.

When these conditions have been met, learner resistance is minimal. The first two conditions are outcomes of an effective training-design process. You can help to meet the third condition during planning and preparation.

In addition to sending an invitation memorandum to learners, it may be advisable for you to meet with or write a memorandum to each learner's supervisor before the program. The purpose of the meeting or memorandum is to encourage supervisors to meet with each of their subordinates who will participate to explain the goals of the program, the reason for attendance, performance expectations after program completion, and how support will be provided. When learners attend with management's encouragement and support, they are more likely to approach the program enthusiastically.

Adults are motivated to learn when they see purpose, meaning, and relevance in the training program. Requiring attendance may cause learners to feel coerced or controlled. Sometimes, of course, required attendance is a must; if that is the case, you and the learners' supervisors must work together to reduce, if not eliminate, the risks of resistance.

SEATING ARRANGEMENTS

Seating is another important consideration in your planning. A good rule of thumb is that "form follows function." First determine the learning goals and then select the form that best contributes to reaching those goals. Seating is not only utilitarian, but can enhance the social climate in which learners gather.

We believe that the fan-type seating arrangement (Figure 2-2) is most conducive to delivering andragogical designs. Although the figure shows tables that seat four or five each, the arrangement could accommodate a smaller or larger group at each table.

The fan-type arrangement offers three main advantages:

1. All learners are afforded a good view of you, as the trainer, and the audiovisual aids.
2. Learners easily can switch from listening to a presentation to working with their subgroups to taking part in a total-group discussion.

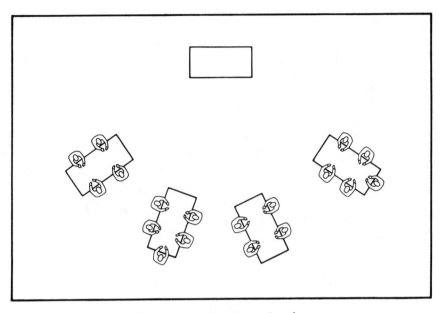

Figure 2-2. Fan-Type Seating

3. It is easy for learners to communicate with one another, even across the room, because everyone's view is relatively unobstructed.

If the learning goal is something other than analysis, synthesis, and judgment, other arrangements are also effective. For example, if the goal is largely knowledge acquisition or awareness—in which presentation, independent completion of work sheets, and audiovisual methods predominate—you may want each table to accommodate two or three learners, with each learner facing in the same direction. This classroom-type configuration is illustrated in Figure 2-3.

If total-group discussion is the predominant method to be used, with limited presentation and/or no subgroup interaction, a conference-table arrangement (Figure 2-4) can be effective. If the program requires both presentation and total-group discussion, the horseshoe-seating arrangement (Figure 2-5) may work well. Both Figure 2-4 and Figure 2-5 picture the training group already involved in the learning.

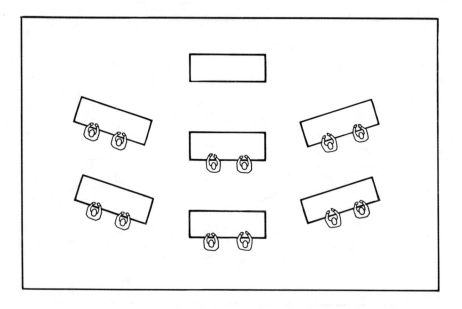

Figure 2-3. Classroom-Type Seating

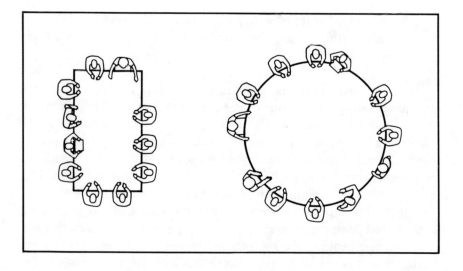

Figure 2-4. Conference-Table Seating

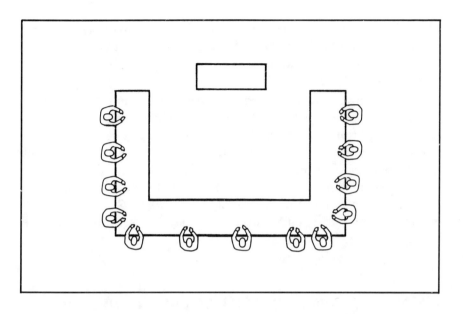

Figure 2-5. Horseshoe Seating

The room should be large enough to accommodate the tables and chairs needed and still allow you adequate space to move around while presenting. Learners also need enough room to work comfortably, store their belongings, and move around occasionally. A cramped room makes everyone feel confined and restless.

The following are some other potential problems and solutions for these problems.

- *Problem:* a room so large that it feels like a cavern. *Solution:* Set up the training in one end or corner of the room, marking a boundary with some sort of room divider, if possible.
- *Problem:* a room with pillars or other obstructions. *Solution:* When arranging the room, make every effort to ensure that all learners can see one another, the visual aids, and you.
- *Problem:* a room filled with distractions, such as elaborate audiovisual equipment, couches, and large paintings. *Solution:* Remove as many distractions as possible and cope with the rest.

(Every trainer has a story about doing training with something like a mounted trophy or a frieze of mermaids competing for the learners' attention.)

A learning environment requiring a special setup is that used for computer-based training (CBT). Figure 2-6 depicts the setup typically used by CBT trainers. The major problem with this setup is the difficulty the trainer has in working with learners individually without major distraction to others.

We recommend that you set up the room for people learning via computer terminals in the manner shown in Figure 2-7. If the group is large (more than twenty learners), it may be useful to set up the room as shown in Figure 2-8.

USING EQUIPMENT AND AUDIOVISUAL AIDS

It is important to remember that the word *aid*, as in audiovisual aid, implies a subordinate or ancillary role. If a training program is built around a particular aid, such as a film, or is totally dependent on a certain piece of equipment to be effective, you risk shifting the emphasis from the learners to the presentation.

The following ideas are offered as general instructions about assembling the equipment and aids that a training program might require. It is recommended that, in addition, you review some of the many excellent books and articles on the use of training equipment. The subject of how to use equipment during a training program is addressed later in this book.

Overhead Projector

Make sure that the glass on the projector is free of smears; otherwise, they will show up on the screen. A lens cloth must be used to clean the glass. (Facial tissues will scratch it.) Some overhead projectors come with a roll of clear acetate on which to write with a grease pencil. If

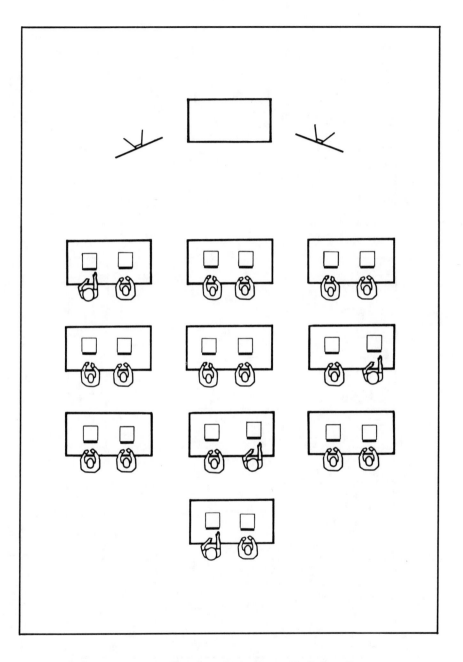

Figure 2-6. Ineffective Computer Training Setup

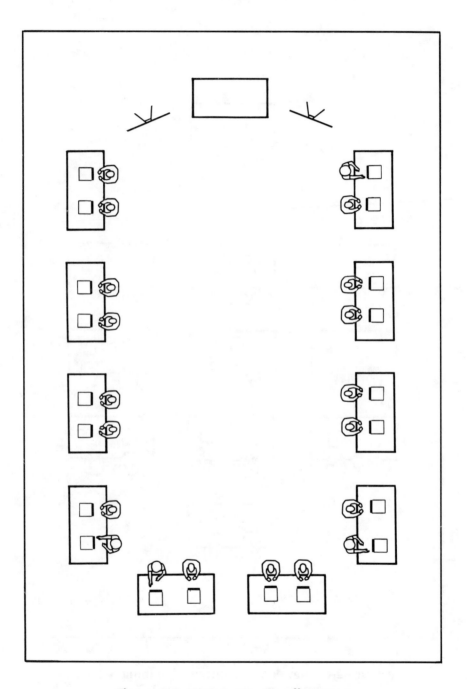

Figure 2-7. CBT Setup (Small Group)

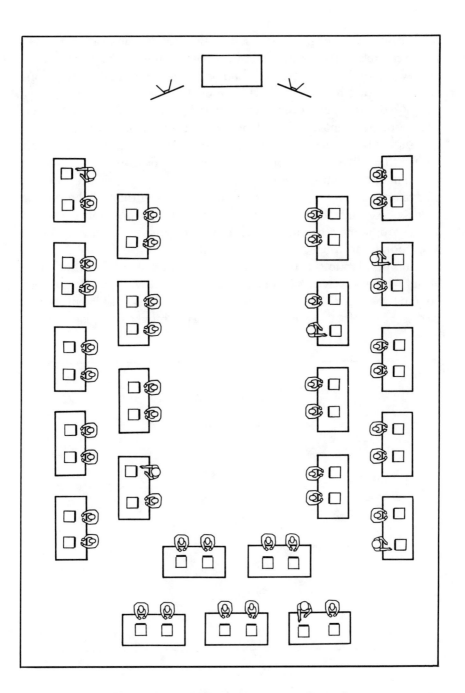

Figure 2-8. CBT Setup (Large Group)

a felt-tipped marker has been used on the acetate, the resulting marks are extremely difficult to erase; but it is possible to buy solvents to remove them. In an emergency, hair spray or some deodorants, along with a lot of elbow grease, will remove felt-tipped-marker jottings.

We suggest positioning an overhead projector so that it projects at a 45-degree angle from the front of the room. Audiovisual research has shown that it is easier to read transparencies projected at an angle rather than directly in front of learners. See Figure 2-9.

Tilt the screen forward at the top, if possible. This prevents the image on the screen from being wider at the top than at the bottom (the Keystone effect). Some portable screens can be positioned forward at the top; some permanent, pull-down screens can be attached near the floor at an angle.

If you plan to set the projector on a rolling stand and then move it out of the way when it is not in use, you will want to put masking tape on the floor where the wheels will rest. This way it will not be necessary to refocus each time the projector is moved into place for use.

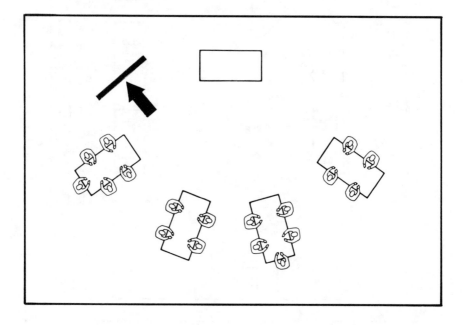

Figure 2-9. Recommended Positioning of an Overhead Projector

And, finally, it is wise to remember this dictum: "An overhead projector is only as good as the bulb." Make sure a spare bulb is always available for any projecting equipment. (Audiovisual professionals refer to bulbs as "lamps.")

Transparencies

It is best if overhead transparencies are professionally prepared. A major factor in producing good transparencies is the readability of words projected on the screen. Although the key variable is the distance from the learner to the screen, a good rule of thumb is to allow no more than seven lines per transparency, seven words per line. You can ensure that everyone is able to see by sitting in the chair that is farthest from the screen and seeing how well you can read the text.

Color enhances visual appeal. Transparencies with color backgrounds (as opposed to clear backgrounds, which project white on the screen) are less tiring to the reader. Key words in different colors heighten interest. The use of too many colors, however, is pure artifice and is distracting. Use your judgment in this matter.

Easel, Newsprint, and Felt-Tipped Markers

An easel pad is usually referred to as a "flip chart" since each page of the pad can be flipped over an easel after it has been used. The paper in the pad is usually called "newsprint." (There was a time when such paper came in rolls from the local newspaper office.)

Easel, newsprint, and felt-tipped markers are useful in highlighting key points during a presentation. Learners can use newsprint and markers with or without easels to record their ideas and thoughts during subgroup tasks. Newsprint can be posted on the walls with masking tape so that learners can review its information during breaks or use it in conjunction with later activities in the program, and it can be saved and its contents typed as a follow-up refresher.

If, on occasion, you have a newsprint pad but no easel, you may be able to hang the pad over a portable chalkboard, with the cardboard backing behind the board and the newsprint sheets in front. One trainer, who had a pad but no easel or chalkboard, draped the pad over the back of a chair stacked on top of a coffee table. This ingenious approach solved the problem. It also is possible to tape individual sheets of newsprint to the walls or windows; the important thing to remember is to use three or four sheets at a time so that the marker will not bleed through.

Start the session with an ample supply of markers on hand, and test each marker before the session begins to make sure that it has not dried up. We suggest using dark colors—black, dark blue, or dark green—because colors such as red, yellow, and orange are difficult to read at a distance and/or are fatiguing to the eye over time.

We suggest using chalkboards instead of newsprint *only* if absolutely necessary. Chalkboards are difficult to read at a distance; they must be erased periodically (unlike newsprint, which can be torn off the pad and taped to the wall for referral and review); and the chalk dust can become messy after several erasings.

Audiovisual Media

Video programs, 16mm films, and 35mm slide presentations are valuable tools in some situations. They are less useful when the goals concern processes that learners must perform, teach others, or supervise, or when the program deals with knowledge that learners must thoroughly understand and apply.

Audiovisual media can be effectively used:

- To illustrate interpersonal skills that would be almost impossible to reproduce live in a classroom without professional actors;
- To establish a situation or incident to which learners can respond;
- To show facilities or events at a remote location;
- To present intricate and hard-to-visualize concepts or processes; and
- To convey a personality or authority. For example, certain companies have produced filmed interviews with their presidents to communicate new policies.

It is important to position all equipment—easel, chalkboard, screen, and so on—so that each learner can read any text easily. Part of your preparation includes sitting in the most distant chair to check readability.

As mentioned earlier, the learning program should not depend solely on an audiovisual aid. Films tear, cassettes jam, bulbs pop, machines break down. If slides are used, you have little flexibility during the session to change the sequence of ideas presented because the slides have already been loaded into a tray in a particular sequence. In addition, with slides, videocassettes, and films, the lights must be dimmed, and dim lights tend to place learners in a passive mode. In short, remember that the human element is the heart of every program, and aids should be just that—helpers and supplements.

Handouts

The preparation of handouts is primarily a design issue. But making sure that you have what is needed during the session is a planning issue. In general, learners like handouts; they enjoy receiving something to take back to the job, to review and digest at their leisure, and to share with colleagues. When planning to use handouts, review program objectives closely, paying particular attention to how the use of handouts might (or might not) enhance learning during and after the session. Distribute readings or articles only if they are directly related to the topic and useful; *more* is not necessarily *better*.

There are three types of handouts:

1. Those that will help learners to follow you as you make a presentation or guide a discussion: topic outlines, models, diagrams, or "structured syllabuses" with a few key words for note taking;
2. Those that are task oriented: the rules and procedures for a game or an exercise, case studies, answer sheets, and so on; and
3. Those that provide learners with continued opportunities for learning after the session: pertinent quotes, bibliographies, reprints of articles, lists of materials, and so on.

If copyrighted material is used, it is essential that you *obtain permission to reprint or to adapt* and *reproduce the credit line exactly as requested by the copyright holder.*

A Clock

One important piece of equipment that trainers often overlook is a timepiece. A small clock (no ticktocks) placed beside your notes will assist you in keeping track of time; such a clock is much more difficult to ignore than a wrist watch. In addition, a clock offers another advantage over a watch: The trainer who looks at a watch switches the learners' attention from the learning to the time.

PROVIDING REFRESHMENTS

Adults are people with set habits. It is important to honor those habits as long as they do not interfere with the learning. Most learners, for instance, expect some type of refreshment.

It is a good idea to provide at least coffee, hot tea, and one caffeine-free beverage for refreshment breaks. Many learners enjoy fruit juice. Soft drinks may be served during an afternoon break, but be sure to include some sugar-free alternatives.

It is preferable to avoid pastries. Research shows that sugar-laden foods have a detrimental effect on one's energy level. Although one experiences a quick surge of energy immediately after eating something like a jelly roll, this effect is followed by a dramatic decrease in energy, which detracts from learning. If learners are accustomed to eating during breaks, one alternative is to offer fruit or cheese or crackers. We are not suggesting that you become card-carrying "health nuts," but we are concerned about the effect that diet has on quality learning.

Be careful with regard to mixing alcoholic drinks with learning. If the organization permits or expects alcoholic drinks to accompany training (particularly off site), provide such drinks after the session only. Like sugar, alcohol dulls the attention needed for effective learning.

Inform learners about whether a meal will be provided before, during, or after the training program. If the training is conducted in two three-hour segments with a meal scheduled between the two segments, plan to serve a light one. Sessions that begin right after a heavy meal often have their share of listless or sleepy learners.

CHECK LIST FOR TRAINING PREPARATION

Because it is vital that you prepare in a number of ways before the training program begins, a preparation check list has been provided (Figure 2-10). With experience, you will want to add your own reminders; consequently, sections for notes have been added to the check list.

Three or More Weeks Before the Training Program:

_____ Select the date of the program.

_____ Select and reserve the site.

_____ Survey the site for size, lighting, ventilation, and furniture needs.

_____ If the training is to be conducted off site, check on transportation arrangements.

_____ Send an invitation memorandum or letter to potential learners. (Include a map if training is to be off site.)

_____ Meet with or call learners' supervisors.

_____ Contact appropriate person about opening and closing site.

_____ Order the necessary number of chairs and tables.

_____ Have handout materials reproduced.

_____ Locate audiovisual equipment and aids.

Figure 2-10. Check List for Training Preparation

Notes:

One Week Before the Training Program:

_____ Confirm number of learners.

_____ Order refreshments.

_____ Decide on smoking policy. Secure ashtrays if necessary.

_____ Obtain direction signs indicating designated room.

_____ Secure a reliable timepiece.

_____ Obtain name tags.

_____ Obtain felt-tipped markers.

_____ Obtain pencils or pens and note pads.

_____ Recheck handouts and aids.

_____ Locate restroom facilities.

Figure 2-10 (continued). Check List for Training Preparation

_____ Recheck equipment arrangements.

_____ Conduct a "dress rehearsal."

_____ Determine and allot time required for setting up materials.

_____ Test all equipment.

Notes:

Day of Training Session (Minimum of One Hour Before Session Begins):

_____ Organize materials on training table.

_____ Make sure that the room is set up properly.

_____ Tape electrical cords to the floor.

_____ Check for spare bulbs.

_____ Make sure that the newsprint pad contains sufficient paper.

Figure 2-10 (continued). Check List for Training Preparation

_____ See that refreshments are in place.

_____ Place note pads, pencils, name tags, and so forth on tables.

_____ Test equipment again.

_____ Ensure that the entrance to the room displays the program title.

_____ Make arrangements for on-site phone coverage and a message-display board.

_____ Ensure that the sound system works and that lighting dimmers have been located.

_____ Post smoking/no-smoking signs if appropriate.

Notes:

Figure 2-10 (continued). Check List for Training Preparation

Additional Considerations

The following list of items is provided to jog your memory; some will be applicable to a particular situation, and some will not. In addition, some are covered in the previous sections of this check list, and some are not.

Film projector
Slide projector
Overhead projector
Films
Screens
Video camera
Video recorder
Television monitor
Videotapes
Audio recorder
Audiotapes
Batteries
Extra flip charts
Extra easels
Extra newsprint pads
Extra markers for writing on newsprint/white board
Markers for writing on transparencies
Blank transparencies
Handouts
Computer terminal
Calculator
Screwdriver
Slides
Overhead transparencies
Three-hole punch
Phone-message pad
Parking permits

Figure 2-10 (continued). Check List for Training Preparation

Pliers
Stapler
Tape (masking/transparent)
Pins
Glue
Chalkboard
Chalk
Meals
Liquid correction fluid ("white-out")
Mail
Hammer
Fee arrangements
Pencil sharpeners
Extension cords
35mm remote extension cord
"Breakout" rooms (for subgroups)
Certificates
Registration materials
Photocopying facilities
Map
Expense forms
Evaluation sheets
Black slides
Three-way adapter
Extra bulbs ("lamps")
First-aid kit
Antacid
Aspirin
Extra note pads and pens
Continuing Education Unit credit forms
Scissors
3" x 5" index cards
String

Figure 2-10 (continued). Check List for Training Preparation

Lens cloth
Matches
Cork screw

Notes:

Figure 2-10 (continued). Check List for Training Preparation

PREPARING ONESELF

A good trainer presents from knowledge rather than memory. It is not advisable to memorize presentations. When you try to remember every line or every fact, one stumble may cause the entire presentation to come unraveled.

If memorizing something seems absolutely necessary, the opening line can be memorized. Nervousness is likely to be at its peak during the first five minutes, so the opening remarks might be prepared thoroughly.

Rehearsal is essential. A tape recorder can help you listen for ways to improve delivery and clarify instructions. An even better method of rehearsing and fostering improvement is to recruit a few friends to serve as an audience. Practice is the path to competence and confidence.

After rehearsing, it is a good idea to stop, relax, and clear your mind. Beginning a training session like an actor in a play or like an automaton, trying to recall the best way in which the training has been delivered previously, can only increase nervousness. Adequate rehearsal allows the program content and sequencing to be internalized; after this point the training is just a matter of instructing as effectively as possible, using your own style and personality.

Always arrive at the training site early. A good rule of thumb is to be on site at least one hour before the session begins. This allows enough time to check to make sure that no gremlins have slipped into the room to upset the arrangements and to set things right if they have. Then the best thing to do is to take a walk, practice deep breathing, or do anything else that helps you reduce internal stress.

Ensure that someone is available to greet learners as they enter the room. Some trainers find that if they perform this function themselves and chat briefly with learners on arrival, presession anxiety can be defused. Others prefer to leave the greeting to others and enter just before the session begins. We suggest doing whatever works best for you and fits your organization.

If nervousness persists in the form of quivering legs or shortness of breath, it is advisable to find a convenient time to pause, reach for a glass of water, take several deep breaths, and flex the leg muscles before continuing. Acknowledging your nervousness is also advisable. Sometimes stage fright is aggravated by trying to hide it. Learners are smart enough to recognize fear when they see it. If you acknowledge you're a little bit nervous at the outset, you can transfer the energy you're spending on hiding this nervousness into managing the session more effectively. Nervousness actually can help, too: It can sharpen and tune your energy to the point where you can be as brilliant as you're capable of being. The trick is to turn nervous energy from a detriment to a benefit.

Chapter 3
Setting and Maintaining
a Learning Climate

One of your primary responsibilities is to establish an atmosphere—often called a "learning climate"—in which people are ready to "dig in and get to work." This does not necessarily mean that every learner is wildly enthusiastic about being in a training session. It does mean, however, that most of those who attend are in an open and cooperative frame of mind, are not unduly distracted, and are serious about doing some work.

Obviously, a good learning climate does not establish itself automatically. It evolves largely in two ways: through the initial activities built into the learning design and through your words and actions.

Most well-designed programs begin with some activity created to foster a good climate for learning. Good climate-setting activities, often called "icebreakers," are designed to facilitate everyone's involvement and relate in some way to the content of the program. We encourage you to avoid subjecting learners to awkward or trivial icebreakers. The climate will not be conducive to learning if learners are asked at the outset to participate in some competitive exercise that they might "fail." Give learners a chance to become comfortable in the situation before plunging into the program content.

Equally important in setting and maintaining an appropriate climate for learning is what you bring to the situation: your voice quality, movement, state of mind, as well as the way you project yourself (with a manner that is formal or informal, precise or easygoing, personal or impersonal). Paying attention to the impact of these intangible qualities goes a long way toward meeting your responsibilities with regard to climate setting.

In most training situations, the best climate is one that projects a sense of controlled informality. A sense of formality or informality is a function of many things: how people are dressed, the nature of the setting, how furniture is arranged in the room, the language that you use, how you treat learners. We believe that most people do not readily experiment or try out new ideas in a rigidly formal setting. This does not imply that the setting must always be informal, however. For example, if the training program is designed to foster the development of skills in doing selection interviews, the learners would probably be dressed in business attire because of the fact that in most organizations this is the dress they will use when interviewing. In this case you may even decide to deliver the program in a location that approximates an actual interviewing situation in order to encourage better transfer of learning. On the other hand, if the training is designed to foster the development of skills in a rather difficult interpersonal area (such as the ability to give corrective feedback), more informal dress and a more relaxed setting might be appropriate to reduce stiffness and encourage exploration of new ideas and behavior.

Whether the setting is formal or informal, it is important that learners feel free to make mistakes and to experiment with ideas and behavior. In a positive learning climate, learners sense that they will not be "punished" for their responses, but that they will be supported as individuals, even though you may suggest possible adjustments in the ways in which they approach certain tasks. It is important that you avoid creating the impression that you know it all and are the ultimate expert. When the learning climate is one of mutual excitement, mutual exploration, and mutual respect, significant learning is more likely to occur.

BEGINNING THE SESSION

Early in the program, describe yourself as a guide, a facilitator, and a catalyst. Inform learners that although you have certain ideas to present, you want them to share their ideas as well. If the climate is described as one of mutual control (rather than trainer control), learners will develop the expectation that they are to take major responsibility for asserting and fulfilling their own learning needs.

Describe the objectives for the training program and provide an overview of how the training time will be managed. All learners appreciate knowing from the start where the session is going, how you envision reaching this point, and what is expected of them. Alert learners regarding when rest and stretch breaks are planned.

Form subgroups early in the session, and give members of subgroups an opportunity to chat among themselves. Learners perform more effectively on subgroup tasks when they have heard the task instructions as a group.

Let learners know how you prefer to handle questions. Some trainers like to hold questions until the end of a presentation to maintain the momentum of the session; others prefer that learners ask questions as they come to mind. Either procedure is acceptable as long as you inform learners of your preference early in the session. Learners also need to know whether they should take notes. If you plan to distribute a handout covering the training content at the end of the session, you may wish to suggest that learners jot only a few notes to themselves to capture important ideas as they occur.

DURING THE SESSION

Before each break briefly review major learnings and plans regarding the work that will immediately follow the break: "After lunch, you'll begin to examine the major ways in which . . . ." This preview helps to maintain forward momentum while bolstering the learners' sense of security and predictability.

Occasionally poll the learners to ascertain the relevance of what they have learned. Such queries or probes can be straightforward: "Is what you are working on useful to you?" The nodding of a few heads is all that is needed to confirm that a climate of learner-focused instruction is being maintained and that you are justified in proceeding.

Model the main characteristics of the learning climate. For instance, if you remove your jacket while asking learners to make themselves comfortable, they will be encouraged to do likewise. If learners are told that they may refill their coffee cups without waiting for a break and then you do so at a convenient time, a climate of trust and psychological comfort is fostered. Many trainers find that occasionally moving among the learners—for example, between subgroups seated at different tables during a total-group discussion—helps to maintain openness and informality.

TRAINER ATTITUDE

The following suggestions are offered as ways in which the trainer can help to foster a comfortable, productive learning climate through the attitude that he or she projects:

Adopt an andragogical perspective to show respect for the learners' individuality and experience.

Be sensitive to your language so that learners are not inadvertently offended.

Be open to different perspectives. The learners in the group will probably have some wonderful new ideas. They may approach things more creatively than you do or than the training design anticipates. Be prepared for this and, if it occurs, enjoy it. If the job of training is performed correctly, each person who attends the session is likely to be learning something at least slightly different, depending on his or her personal needs, experience, and current situation. Avoid approaching the session with the idea that all learners must learn exactly what you think they should learn. Instead, view the training experience as a cooperative venture for learning.

Adopt a caring attitude and show it. This means showing concern about the learners as people in addition to demonstrating concern about their learning. It also means not treating them as vessels into which knowledge is poured.

Treat the learners as individuals rather than as a group of people who are all alike. The learners are not a "class" to be taught; they are a group of competent people seeking to increase their knowledge and competence with your help.

Support all learner comments by acknowledging the "rightness" that is in each comment and each person. This does not mean that wrong answers are right. It means that exploration, effort, personal integrity, creativity, and risk taking should be supported. Thoughts, ideas, or answers that are inaccurate can be identified for what they are without demeaning the people who voiced them.

Take the learning process seriously because it is serious and important. It is an experience to be valued and one that you help the learners to value. On the other hand, don't take yourself too seriously. Granted, you are an important person doing important work; however, if your attitude bespeaks superiority, pedantry, or righteousness, it will interfere with learning. In contrast, an attitude that reflects hopefulness, humility, wonderment, searching, and enjoyment will improve the climate immensely.

Describing these approaches is easier than adopting them. The best trainers try to be caring and supportive, to treat learners as individuals, and to take the process (rather than themselves) seriously. Figure 3-1 presents some of the major differences between the "controlling" attitude of a teacher and the "discovering" attitude of a trainer. Reviewing this figure may help you to identify your attitude toward instructing. If you discover that you identify more strongly with the teacher attitude, this does not necessarily mean that you are "wrong" or "bad." However, it may mean that such an attitude will direct the climate away from learner-directed discovery and toward teacher-directed transmission of content. We believe that a trainer's attitude can incorporate elements from both controlling and discovering, but is best if skewed toward that of discovering.

THE TRAINER'S LANGUAGE

The language you use can be either controlling or facilitating. The distinction is sometimes difficult to recognize. It is even harder to change one's habitual word choices. Most of us have had educational experiences in which the teacher was totally in charge. In grade school, high school, college, and even graduate school, teachers frequently use controlling language. It is difficult to keep from unconsciously copying this model.

In andragogical training we have found that it is more effective to use facilitating language. Helping people to learn is a very subtle

"Controlling" (Teacher) Attitude	"Discovering" (Trainer) Attitude
Smothering	Concerned
Annoyed	Attentive
Waiting to make a point	Truly interested
Impatient	Encouraging
Seeing group patterns	Seeing individual differences
Responding to group requests	Understanding indiv' lual concerns
Desiring to correct inaccurate comments	Seeking reasons for inaccurate comments
Telling his or her experience	Jointly exploring
Cleverly channeling learners' responses toward "rightness"	Comfortable with learners' seemingly unrelated comments
Proving his or her point	Exploring issues

Figure 3-1. Teacher Attitude Versus Trainer Attitude

process; part of this subtlety comes across in the language one uses. It is difficult to describe the difference between controlling and facilitating language; the critical factor is not necessarily the words used but the way in which they are said and the assumptions they communicate. Most people who use controlling language or tones do so because it is simply a habit.

If you tend to use controlling language in front of a group, you may find that changing this habit takes time and practice. A colleague may need to be recruited to help you to recognize the effects of such language. If possible, tape yourself on videotape or audiotape and ask a colleague to critique the language used.

Here are some cautions regarding language:

Be careful about using the royal "we." For example, a trainer might say, "Now *we* are going to analyze the case." In this instance the use of "we" may sound patronizing or pushy to learners.

Avoid embarrassing or humiliating the learners—in word, tone of voice, or body language, or by not recognizing their work or not acknowledging them as persons.

Avoid giving learners the impression that they are receiving a dictum. Requests are best if based not on your personal desires ("Now I want you to look at page 5"), but on the needs of the program and on the group as a whole ("It's time to reconvene as a group and move on to the next activity"). Facilitating language *welcomes* learners to the activities.

Never use language, humor, or anecdotes that might offend any group of people, such as women, ethnic groups, or disabled people. Even if these groups are not represented in the training group, some learners are likely to be offended and, consequently, to "turn off" to both the program and the user.

HANDLING RESISTANCE

In most organizations and in most situations, people come into a training session to learn, willingly and eagerly. But sometimes a trainer may encounter resistance from one or more learners.

Signs of resistance include:

- Excessive questioning on the part of learners who are trying to make a point rather than gain knowledge;
- Numerous side conversations between or among learners;
- Perfunctory participation in group tasks;
- Questions aimed at trapping or baffling the trainer;
- Learners who appear to be sleepy when they are not really fatigued;
- A refusal to participate;
- Disruptive and/or inappropriate behavior; and
- Questions that challenge the relevance of the training and/or the competence of the trainer.

The biggest trap for you to avoid is that of employing methods that most of us experienced in grade school. In that environment resistance was met by threat ("If you don't get quiet, I'm going to . . . ") or sarcastic accommodation ("We'll all wait until Johnny decides to join us").

When you encounter resistance, your first task is to discover its cause. The cause may be a learner's perception that he or she is being controlled, coerced, or manipulated by you or the program. However, it is more likely that the cause has little to do with you and instead relates to experiences outside the training. Discovering the cause for learner resistance better enables you to adjust, cope, and solve problems. Most resistance is attributable to one or more of the following causes:

1. People have been sent to the training session
   - inappropriately.
   - when they are too busy.
2. Learners do not understand
   - why the program is relevant to them.
   - why the program is important to their jobs.
   - why they were selected to attend.
3. Outside influences are interfering, such as
   - concerns about family, money, or health.
   - problems with a superior or subordinate.
4. Emotional issues are interfering, such as
   - negative past experiences with training programs.
   - disruptive interpersonal behavior that is characteristic of a particular learner (for example, an intense need for attention or a need to dominate).

We suggest the following four-step process for dealing with resistance:

1. *Look inward.* Ask yourself the following questions:
   - Could anything I am doing or saying be construed as controlling?
   - Is my attitude one of supportiveness?

2. *Consult.*
   - Find out why the learners think they are present.
   - Find out what would make the training useful.
3. *Offer opportunities for learner reactions.*
   - Find out what is not meaningful to them.
   - Provide an opportunity for venting fears, frustrations, anger, and so on.
   - Elicit the learners' help in determining how the learning could be made more meaningful.
4. *Confront directly.*
   - Speak to disruptive learners during a break and solicit their support.
   - If all else fails and someone persists in interfering with the learning of others, ask the disruptive person to leave. At the first opportunity, tell this individual's supervisor why he or she was asked to leave.

Not all learners will always agree with the philosophy of the training program. However, our experience is that such problems arise far less frequently than new trainers may anticipate. When such problems develop, you will likely be able to solve them in your own way.

Chapter 4
Making Presentations

The art of making presentations in a training session differs considerably from the art of making speeches. In most speeches the focus is on "serving up" information that frequently is laced with humor, entertaining anecdotes, and/or exhortations of various sorts. In training presentations, however, the emphasis is on learning. As a trainer, therefore, concentrate on what is *learned* rather than on what is *taught*. Even when you plan to deliver only a short speech, the dynamics of the situation—the context, the purpose, and the mental set of the learners—dictate that the message be delivered quite differently from the way it would be in a formal speech-making situation.

THE IMPORTANCE OF BEING NATURAL

We believe that your ability to be natural and to express your own personality is the most important skill in making effective presentations. Whatever you do while making a presentation—whether delivering a short lecture or performing a demonstration—it is essential to be yourself. If you have a tendency to pace around the room a bit while speaking, this habit is perfectly acceptable as long as you focus on the people who are listening. Ending sentences with prepositions is perfectly acceptable if this is your natural way of speaking. Having a cup of coffee during a training session is acceptable as long as the learners can do the same. Similarly, standing fairly straight or rigidly when in front of learners or sitting on the edge of a table is acceptable if the position is comfortable for you.

Our advice to be yourself in a training situation does not mean that "anything goes." Some behaviors, like smoking cigarettes or avoiding contact by staring at the ceiling, can undermine your ability to help people to learn, even if these behaviors are natural for you. Strive to express your personality in a way that is natural, but minimize inappropriate behaviors that distract the learners.

Such behaviors are usually a function of nervousness and generally fall into one of two categories: *audible* behaviors and *visible* behaviors. Audible behaviors include clicking a pen, coughing, clearing one's throat, and frequent use of verbal tics such as "you know" and "okay." Certain visible behaviors also can be distracting. Smoking cigarettes and staring at the ceiling, as mentioned before, are only two of these behaviors; there are probably thousands more. Rhythmic swaying can be distracting, and so can pacing around the room like a lion in a cage.

The question of what to do with your hands is also important, but it becomes more of a problem when you focus on it. Keeping your hands in your pockets is acceptable as long as you do not jingle change. It is equally acceptable to keep your hands folded in front of your body as long as you are attentive and maintain good eye contact so that this posture does not seem defensive.

Many trainers occupy their hands in ways that work well in conjunction with their training designs. Probably the most common is holding a felt-tipped marker. You can fiddle with it unobtrusively, use it as a pointer, and even *write* with it! However, avoid using a long pointer; its disadvantage is the tendency to wave it around like a swagger stick or to jab it aggressively at the learners.

Fingers do not make good pointers, either. When gesturing to an individual or subgroup—for example, when asking whether a subgroup is ready to report—keep your hand open and your palm turned up. This gesture creates a friendlier, more accepting feeling than does a pointed finger.

MAINTAINING CONTACT

When making a presentation, it is important that you make and keep as much contact with the learners as possible, both physically and psychologically. It is your job to help people to learn and to help them to feel comfortable about learning; it is not your job to teach, to dictate to the learners, or to try to control them. Instead, enter into partnership with the learners in the learning experience. This partnership evolves much more readily when there are no barriers between you and the learners.

Physical Contact

The best position from which to project your voice, to see all the learners, and to hold their attention is a standing position. You may be more comfortable sitting; however, if you sit behind a table, you may find it difficult to maintain eye contact with the whole group. Many trainers find sitting on the edge of a table to be a good alternative. This position is a comfortable one, and it conveys an attitude of relaxed attention.

Most trainers like to sit during group-discussion periods, when there is no reason for them to be the center of attention. In such cases, sit beside or in front of the table. The important point to remember is that the possibility of creating physical barriers or boundaries between you and the learners should be at least reduced as much as possible, if not eliminated.

Another important consideration is where to put notes. You can hold them in your hands or put them on a table nearby. Know the training design and material well enough so that you only have to refer to notes occasionally and casually. Overhead transparencies or outlines on newsprint can also help you to remember the key points in the presentation.

Psychological Contact

You can maintain psychological contact in several ways. For example, you can mix with the learners during breaks or move through the room unobtrusively as they are working.

The best speakers emphasize the use of eye contact to make the listeners feel that the speaker is interested in them. This practice also works in training. You *need* to make eye contact to know what's happening, how learners are reacting, what they agree and disagree with, what they understand and what they are confused about.

PACE AND TONE

When presenting, establish a pace and tone that are natural for you. Some presenters work best in a somewhat formal atmosphere, and some prefer informality. The important thing is for you to become increasingly aware of what your own style is and how it works best to facilitate learning. Once these stylistic factors are understood, you can use them effectively. If handling interruptions when they occur works well for you, encourage learners to interrupt whenever they feel the necessity. On the other hand, if waiting until the end of a presentation to handle questions and comments works better, inform the learners of this personal preference.

Using Humor

In training, humor is a tool that is brilliant when used well and disastrous when used poorly. Often the brilliant applications are spontaneous, while the disasters have been too carefully planned. Everyone has heard a trainer start a session by telling a bad joke poorly; usually the joke has nothing to do with the training session and is told only to "warm up" the learners. Instead, it leaves them cold—and the trainer embarrassed and uneasy.

Our recommendation is not to make a specific effort to be funny. Most trainers are not top-notch comedians. However, if you are naturally witty and can see the humor in a particular training situation, capitalize on it and share it with the learners. The exception is humor that denigrates people, such as that which is common at a "roast." It may be funny to some, but it will create a destructive climate that will offend everyone in the long run. For the person for whom humor does not come naturally, it is not a good idea to try to develop it while training. A well-prepared training session will be excellent with or without humor.

Using "Bells and Whistles"

You do not need figurative "bells and whistles" to make a presentation effective. It is not even necessary to use a half-dozen different colored markers on a sheet of newsprint. Insecure trainers sometimes use tricks and trappings to try to capture learners' attention. Sometimes they use these devices just to show off. Whatever their motives, these trainers would do well simply to deliver their programs directly, honestly, and clearly. The "bells and whistles" are gimmicks; at best they do not interfere, and at worst the learners remember the gimmicks at the expense of learning the content.

USING MATERIALS AND AIDS

Although "bells and whistles" are not recommended, a trainer often does need certain materials and aids to support a presentation. The best general advice is to practice giving the presentation in advance, rehearsing when and how the supporting materials will be used.

Notes and Outlines

It is critical that notes and outlines not control you. While preparing for a presentation, outline the major points and subpoints. The problem with writing out notes word for word is that you may be tempted to read them. In contrast, a topical outline will help you to add your own personality and ideas to the communication process without being tied to a prepared text.

There is no need to hide the fact that notes are being used. However, since they are aids only, use them sparingly. Handle notes so that neither you nor the audience is distracted by their use. If you gesture assertively and try to hold notes at the same time, it can be extremely distracting to learners; the result has been cleverly termed the "fly-swat technique." In addition, holding notes at eye level not only encourages you to read them but also creates a barrier between you and the learners.

Overhead Projectors and Transparencies

Although overhead projectors and transparencies are easy to use, many trainers have problems with them. The following are some tips on how to avoid such problems.

- Stand away from the screen.
- Use a sharp pencil to point on the transparency itself; the pencil point will show up on the screen.
- Leave the lights on. Overhead transparencies can be seen well in a regularly lighted room. A darkened room creates an atmosphere in which people sit back and listen passively, whereas a positive training atmosphere is one in which people are closely involved with the content, one another, and the trainer. However, lights can be dimmed slightly if desired.
- Keep the transparencies in order and in focus.
- Be sure that the projector is positioned so that the transparencies can be seen by all learners. After measuring the required height of the screen and the distance from the projector to the screen, put a piece of masking tape on the floor at the appropriate spot so that the projector can be positioned quickly.
- Place each transparency on the glass before turning on the projector. Look at the screen once to make sure that the transparency is positioned correctly; then try not to look at it again. Direct all energy to the learners. Turn the projector off before removing the transparency. Be sure to move the projector when all transparencies have been shown. *Do not* leave the machine in front of the learners unless it is in use; it can be a distraction and a barrier.

Films and Slides

Learner passivity is the greatest danger associated with using films and slides. Because lights must be dimmed at least one-third for slides and two-thirds for films, there is an implicit request for learners to be passive. Films and slides are most effective when they follow or precede an exercise.

Handouts

From a presentation standpoint, the biggest issue regarding handouts is when to distribute them. Some trainers prefer to distribute all handouts early in a training program, and this practice has certain advantages. For example, the trainer who distributes everything early minimizes the break in his or her momentum by simply asking learners to turn to a specific page rather than distributing handouts at several different times.

However, this practice also presents disadvantages. When handouts are distributed early, learners tend to read ahead and risk becoming confused about the trainer's explanation. Similarly, learners may read a handout while the trainer is giving task instructions and miss vital points needed for task completion.

We prefer to distribute handouts as they are needed by the learners, despite the impact on momentum and the added administrative burden. However, you should decide what works best for you.

Newsprint

Newsprint is a powerful tool when used well, but boring and a waste of time when used poorly. After something has been recorded on a sheet of newsprint, the sheet can be taped in the front of the room if that particular material is being used at the moment. Sheets of newsprint containing information that learners need to refer to occasionally, such as an agenda, can be taped to the side walls. Newsprint information already covered that learners might want to review during a break or to use as background or resource material can be posted in the back of the room. During breaks, reposition or remove sheets of newsprint as necessary so that the room does not become cluttered.

The intelligent, creative use of newsprint can add a great deal to a training program. There are three distinctly different ways to use it.

As a Substitute for Slides or Transparencies

Newsprint can be used instead of slides or transparencies as the presentation medium. Write important items on a sheet of newsprint in outline form before making the presentation. This sheet then serves as a reference list for both you and the learners. A second sheet of newsprint can be used to block the items not yet discussed; in this case you simply tape the second sheet in place over the first sheet, repositioning it to uncover items as the presentation proceeds.

Using this approach allows the newsprint to be prepared in advance so that all items can be neatly arranged and presented precisely as you want them. In addition, you can maintain your position in front of the learners without having to turn away from them to write. If you elect not to block any items, an additional advantage is that the learners can anticipate what is coming next in the presentation.

However, preparing newsprint in advance also presents certain disadvantages. This approach can appear overly structured and inflexible. It also can develop an atmosphere in which the learners perceive you as the talker and themselves as only listeners. In addition, unless you block items not yet discussed, the learners will read ahead instead of concentrating on what you are saying.

As a Way to Emphasize Concepts During the Session

You can record key words and concepts on newsprint while presenting rather than before the session. This approach is dramatic and allows quite a bit of flexibility. For example, you can change the order in which ideas are presented, if necessary. The main disadvantage is that unless you write quickly, the writing process itself will take a lot of time; on the other hand, if the writing is done too quickly, the results will look sloppy and scrawled and may lack other elements of precision.

As a Means of Recording Learners' Comments

This can be a useful technique when learners make reports on a subgroup exercise and you wish to organize or categorize the items mentioned. However, be careful not to overuse this method. The unnecessary recording of information can be tedious and redundant and can distract from the learning. Record information on newsprint only when one or more of the following conditions apply:

- Emphasis is necessary;
- The information will be referred to later; and
- All recorded items are necessary for the purpose of synthesis, conceptualization, model building, or review.

MANAGING TIME

As you present, you may find that the pre-existing training instructions called for a fifteen-minute presentation but everything has been said in nine or ten minutes. In this situation it is a good idea to check whether the learners have generally understood the principles and ideas discussed; if so, proceed and do not repeat any information. It is not necessary to fill the time in exactly the manner prescribed.

On the other hand, you may find that the schedule calls for fifteen minutes and the presentation requires twenty or twenty-five. If you are running that far behind without having answered a lot of learner questions, you are probably being repetitive and may be losing the learners' attention.

Another frequently encountered situation with regard to time management is one in which a stimulating discussion is going on and you think it is useful to the learning to let it continue beyond its prescribed time limit. Feel free to do so, but remember that time will have to be deleted from some other segment to compensate.

Our advice is not to be rigid about time. The decision to adjust any part of the program for a slightly longer or shorter time is up to you, and it is an important part of your responsibility to make effective adjustments.

PRESENTATION TIPS

The more familiar you are with the content of the presentation, the more confident and effective you will be in helping people to learn. Of course, you need to know the content of the instructor's manual that is being used, but you also need to study and extend the ideas in the manual and combine them with your personal experiences, examples, and illustrations. Working with the ideas in this way and developing a sense of ownership about them enables you to deliver a more powerful, helpful presentation.

The following tips are offered as a review of the content of this chapter.

- Avoid cliches and jargon.
- Avoid distracting the learners. Using audiovisual aids that are unrelated to the topic being discussed may break their concentration.
- Do not take yourself too seriously. If you acknowledge your humanity, the learners will be inclined to do likewise.
- Maintain eye contact with learners in all sectors of the room.
- Announce two-minute stretch breaks whenever they seem needed.
- Once a point has been covered adequately, summarize it and move on. Restate essential points frequently to reinforce the continuity of the presentation design.
- Use pauses to let important points sink in and to encourage audience reaction.
- Avoid distracting body language, such as shifting weight from one foot to the other or constantly folding and unfolding arms.
- Never make excuses for elements missing from the session. Excuses call unnecessary attention to imperfections.
- When writing on a flip chart, try not to turn away from the learners. Instead, try standing to the right of the flip chart if you are right-handed and to the left if you are left-handed. In this way your body will not cover the written material.
- Do not talk to the flip chart. Direct your energy toward the learners.
- During breaks move materials or equipment, check your notes or outline to review the next step, and be receptive to comments from learners. But do not become so involved in a conversation that you fail to start on time.
- Avoid stories or language that might offend any member of the group.
- Be yourself. This is the most valuable tip of all.

Learning involves personal risk. People have invested many years in the process of learning to be as they are. When they begin to learn new skills, ideas, and attitudes, they are frequently awkward in the beginning. Such awkwardness can be embarrassing and uncomfortable, particularly when experienced in the presence of others. Your commitment to authenticity—to being the person that you really are—helps to create a climate in which it is safe for learners to take risks. Similarly, your support, both verbal and nonverbal, encourages learners to gain greater confidence and competence as they move from awkward beginnings to accomplished proficiency.

Chapter 5

Giving Instructions

Discovery learning occurs more through the learners' investigation of important issues in structured activities than through trainer presentations. This means that the trainer frequently must give directions for such activities. If the learners do not clearly understand the instructions or if they consider the task unreasonable, the learning process will be disrupted.

Giving effective task instructions demands precision and thoughtfulness. This chapter provides a step-by-step guide for giving instructions and explains why each step in the recommended task-instruction sequence is so important. We urge you to take the time needed to practice this crucial skill until it comes naturally.

A FOUR-STEP GUIDE FOR GIVING TASK INSTRUCTIONS

In developing our ability to instruct, we have identified a powerful principle: Begin all task instructions with the rationale for the task. By explaining the rationale first, you are better able to maintain a climate in which people are motivated to learn.

The following four-step procedure is recommended for giving instructions.

1. *Introduce the task by giving a rationale.* Explain, from the learners' point of view, *why* the learning they are about to acquire could be important to them. The rationale helps learners prepare themselves to work.

2. *Explain the task.* Describe the activity in which the learners will participate to accomplish the learning goal that was explained in the rationale. The task description tells them *what* they will do.

3. *Specify the context.* This information tells learners specifically *how* they will do the work.

4. *Explain what reports are to be made.* After subgroup or individual work, learners are frequently expected to report the results of their work to the entire group.

This sequence follows the logic of learning and the logic of motivation. Avoid using the logic of administration, which follows a sequence of telling learners what they should do and how they should do it before telling them why they should complete the task. Most people have experienced training programs in which trainers introduce a task by saying something like "I'm going to break you into subgroups." Leading with a statement like that generally has a negative effect on learners. They begin looking around the room to identify people they might like to work with, and they may begin feeling apprehensive about the activity before they even know what it is. In addition, learners often have an aversion to working in small subgroups, perhaps because this type of work requires a different kind of effort from sitting and listening.

However, by beginning with a statement of the rationale, you can circumvent this resistance. Learners can see from the outset why the task will be appropriate and valuable. Then when you describe the activity that will accomplish the learning and the conditions or constraints imposed on performing the activity, you help learners to discover that subgroup work is a relevant and useful tool for their learning rather than an irritating, useless exercise.

Many trainers find this sequence difficult to follow at first. They often want to add extraneous comments. We recommend that you avoid this tendency and instead follow the four-step process as closely as possible. In the previous chapter you were cautioned not to read from notes or an outline and instead to make presentations in which your own personality and unique approach are evident. Giving instructions, however, is different. It is imperative that the proper relationship between the learners and their work be established, and this will happen if you follow the four steps in order, reading from notes or a short outline.

Step 1: Giving the Introduction/Rationale

The introduction/rationale is a statement that answers a fundamental question for the learner: "Why should I enter into this task or experience?" It does not answer the question "What exactly will I be doing?" That question is answered in the next step, the description of the task. Only when the learners see a personal benefit from completing the task will they be ready to accept the task assignment. A premature task description can result in overt rejection of the task or superficial acceptance (complying with the "teacher"). Figure 5-1 offers a sample introduction/rationale statement.

The rationale is always stated from the *learner's* perspective, not the trainer's or the organization's perspective. Notice how the rationale presented in Figure 5-2, which is based on the organization's perspective, is less appealing than the rationale offered in Figure 5-1.

"When interviewing someone for a job, you may or may not choose to reveal certain things about yourself or the organization. What is important is that you feel comfortable and competent in revealing certain information to the person being interviewed. This feeling comes with experience. The more we risk, the better we become at taking risks. In a moment you will have an opportunity to practice revealing certain kinds of information."

Figure 5-1. Sample Introduction/Rationale from the Learner's Perspective

---

"When interviewing someone for a job, you may or may not choose to reveal certain things about yourself or the organization. At Acme, we believe you should know in advance what you will reveal before you begin an interview. In a moment you will have the opportunity to practice revealing information."

Figure 5-2. Sample Introduction/Rationale from the Organization's Perspective

The rationale statement should communicate a personal reason for completing the task as well as a professional reason. The reason presented should be one with which the learners can identify, one that makes logical as well as emotional sense. It should not be a justification by the trainer in terms of the training program or the needs of the organization.

The best way to determine whether the rationale is making sense to learners is to look around at them while stating it. Affirmative nodding and attentive looks mean that the statement is on target. On the other hand, stony faces and glazed eyes probably mean that the statement has told the learners what they will do, not why the task is important to them.

It is essential that you understand the purpose, the impact, and the approach of the introduction/rationale. Developing this understanding can be treated as a foreign-language exercise: Try to learn not only to *state* a rationale but also to *think* in the language of the rationale.

Step 2: Explaining the Task

An effective task explanation is constructed so that an individual or group inevitably produces a product. The task statement always incorporates action verbs. Learners should be asked to *list, identify, solve, rank,* and so on. Avoid asking them to discuss, go over, review, think about, or talk about.

In addition to describing the product, the task statement usually includes some phrase that defines the quantity and/or quality expected in the product, such as "list *the most important,*" "list *the five most important,*" or "list *those that you have used.*" Such qualifiers are critical because they enable the task statement to zero in on the exact objective that you have determined is appropriate for a particular kind of learning.

Figure 5-3 presents a sample task explanation. Notice how this statement presents a natural connection between the rationale and the task. Usually there is a transitional sentence; sometimes it is located in the rationale, sometimes in the task explanation. While practicing giving instructions, work on making the transition from the introduction/rationale to the task explanation smooth and complete.

"To help clarify these points, identify and list the most important reasons, in your opinion, that feedback based on performance standards can help employees to do their work more effectively."

Figure 5-3. Sample Task Explanation

Step 3: Defining the Context

The definition of context explains how the learners will accomplish the task. The context for the task involves three elements:

- The size of the working unit (individuals or subgroups);
- The composition of the subgroups, if they are used; and
- The amount of time allotted for completing the task.

Size of the Working Unit

The size of the working unit involved is determined by the nature of the task. The more technical the task and the more it requires individual or personal thought, the smaller the recommended subgroup. Tasks requiring the exploration of ideas and joint creativity are usually designed for groups of four or five.

You may have to adjust this number, depending on the total number of learners in the training session. It may be necessary to create a few subgroups of six. When this happens you need to be particularly attentive to these larger subgroups. Six people often subdivide into two groups of three or even pair off when the work begins. If the size of the entire group at the session is relatively small, it may be more desirable to assemble subgroups of four instead of five or six. Activities designed for subgroups larger than six are uncommon, unless the content of the program is group dynamics. Occasionally you may want to use subgroups of three—usually when the task is somewhat technical but requires the exploration of ideas, or when the task requires two people to do something and a third person to function as an observer (for example, in a role play).

Whether purchased or developed in house, most training designs recommend a particular size of subgroup for each activity, based on a number of carefully considered factors. We recommend you not alter the recommended size of subgroups solely because of the total number of learners in the room. Often the most significant learning happens in subgroups. Therefore, the *size* of the subgroups is far more important than the total number of subgroups working on any given task.

Subgroup Composition

The composition of the subgroups is just as important as their size in accomplishing learning. To understand the effects of subgroup composition, consider the concepts of homogeneity and heterogeneity: Subgroups can be composed of people who are alike or different, according to the objectives of the task.

Homogeneous groups are composed of:

- People who know one another;
- People with the same level of experience;
- People on an equal standing in the organizational hierarchy;
- People who work in the same plant or facility; and/or
- People with the same type of job.

Heterogeneous groups are composed of:

- People who are strangers;
- People with less experience and people with more experience;
- People from different levels in the hierarchy;
- People with different styles of leadership;
- People from different plants or facilities; and
- People with different jobs.

Subgroup composition plays a key role in establishing a good learning climate at the beginning of the session. As a general rule, we recommend that for the first (climate-setting) activity, learners be grouped with others they know least well. This practice offers the following advantages:

- It exposes learners to new ideas from new people.
- It helps learners to avoid habitual patterns of behavior (such as joking around with good friends) that might delay or interfere with learning.
- It keeps learners from evading the task or accomplishing it in a perfunctory way.
- It helps learners to meet others with whom they may want to work or develop a support system.
- It decreases potential competition among those who work together.

Toward the end of a session, it is a good idea to assemble subgroups composed of people who work together so that they can discuss the learning and explore ways to apply what they learned to their own work situation.

Many purchased programs suggest the composition of subgroups that is appropriate for each task, but you should feel free to make adjustments based on the people who will be attending the training session and what will help them to learn in the most effective way. However, you might want to avoid actually forming the subgroups; instead, you can state the criteria for subgroup composition and then allow the learners to organize themselves into subgroups based on those criteria. When you set up subgroups, learners may feel manipulated or may be suspicious about the reasons for putting certain people together.

Time

The amount of time allotted to accomplish a task is important for reasons that may not be obvious at first. This part of task instruction is more an indication of how to do the task than a precise measure of how much time to take; learners understand the nature of the task better when they know about how long they have to accomplish it. If, for example, learners were asked to list as many reasons for something as possible and they were told that they had five minutes to do so, they would know that you expected something like a quick brainstorm. However, if they were given twenty-five minutes to accomplish the same task, they would know that the task involved exploring and analyzing different aspects of the issue. Specifying the amount of time adds a helpful qualifier to the task by focusing energy in a productive way.

In most purchased programs, the amount of time to be stated in instructions is indicated in the trainer's notes. However, as the learners work on the task, you may find that they are finishing early or that they need more time; what to do in this situation is covered in detail on page 79 in Chapter 6, Monitoring Subgroup and Individual Tasks.

Step 4: Explaining What Is to Be Reported

The process of reporting information generated in subgroups adds greatly to individual learning. The goal is not simply to reiterate for the total group what occurred in the subgroups. Instead, the goal is to extend and amplify learning beyond what was gained in the subgroups. Some trainers refer to this as "processing"; others label it "sharing." We call it "reporting." Regardless of the label, you should keep in mind that the intent is to help learners to expand, integrate, and generalize learning from their individual or subgroup work.

When you are giving task instructions and reach the point of explaining what is to be reported, simply tell learners what they are responsible for reporting to the total group when their subgroup work has been completed. This statement does not need to explain *how* you will administratively manage the reporting process when the time comes. Stating the administrative details has a tendency to confuse rather than clarify; in addition, in providing such details you may describe a procedure that you later want or need to alter. Figure 5-4 offers a sample explanation of what is to be reported. Notice that the sample does not mention that the trainer's plan is to ask for only the top three items of each list generated.

"Appoint a spokesperson in your subgroup who will be responsible for sharing your subgroup's list with the total group."

Figure 5-4. Sample Explanation of What Is to Be Reported

Most often, what is to be reported is identical to the task product (or at least a portion of the task product). Sometimes, however, the product of the task is not reported, particularly if it involves personal information that is difficult to disclose. When this is true, be sure to include beforehand a clear statement about what is expected—or not expected—to be shared. Figure 5-5 presents a sample explanation of what is not to be reported.

Occasionally the goal of the task or activity may be such that there is a difference between the product and what is reported. This may occur in certain management-skills training such as that dealing with leadership or group dynamics. For instance, the task may require a subgroup to assemble a Tinkertoy® tower and then have learners report on how the leadership of the subgroup evolved. Similarly, the members of a subgroup may be requested to put together a complex puzzle without talking or touching puzzle pieces other than their own and then to report on their feelings during the task. However, such occasions are the exceptions rather than the rule.

"You will not be asked to share the exact content of what you've written. Writing your ideas will simply help you collect your thoughts so that you can contribute more significantly during the discussion."

Figure 5-5. Sample Explanation of What Is Not to Be Reported

FOUR WAYS TO GIVE TASK INSTRUCTIONS

There are four main ways to give instructions. Each serves a slightly different purpose, but all four give the learners the same information. The choice of method depends on a variety of factors, including:

- How familiar the learners are with the process of listening to instructions for a subgroup task;
- The complexity of the task; and
- The nature of the task.

1. The Basic Pattern

The basic pattern is the type of task instruction used most frequently. It is simply the four elements of a task instruction stated in the proper order. Figure 5-6 offers a sample of the basic pattern.

Give the introduction/rationale. "You have looked at several important principles to follow in delegating work to employees. There are occasions when work delegated is not subsequently performed. Before taking action as a supervisor on such an occasion, it is important that you understand the reasons for the failure of your delegation."

Explain the task. "Recall a time when you delegated work that was not subsequently performed. Write three reasons that this might have occurred."

Specify the context. "Take five minutes to do this individually."

Explain what is to be reported. "Be ready to share your incident, as well as the potential reasons for it, with the total group."

Figure 5-6. Sample of the Basic Pattern of Giving Instructions

2. Shorthand Form

The authors recommend using a shorthand form of instructions when giving them a second time as a summary. If instructions are given a second time quickly and succinctly, the repetition is effective rather than pedantic. Obviously, the shorthand form should never be the only instructions given. Note that the introduction/rationale is omitted from the sample shorthand form provided in Figure 5-7.

3. Instructions Plus Example

The third way to give instructions is to provide the basics followed by an example. This is particularly useful when the task may be somewhat unfamiliar and an example serves to clarify it without doing the work for the learners. After giving the example, you may restate the instructions in shorthand if desired. Figure 5-8 offers a sample of instructions plus an example.

4. Instructions Plus Handout

The fourth way involves first giving the instructions in their usual order. Then, distribute a handout describing the task (or display this information on a flip chart or a transparency). We recommend that instructions be given this way when the task is particularly complicated or has several parts and learners need to refer to written instructions as they work on the task. Figure 5-9 presents a sample of this method.

"Recall a delegation that failed, and write three possible reasons. Take five minutes working alone and be ready to share your results."

Figure 5-7. Sample of the Shorthand Form of Giving Instructions

Give the introduction/rationale. "You have looked at several important principles to follow in delegating work to employees. There are occasions when work delegated is not subsequently performed. Before taking action as a supervisor on such an occasion, it is important that you analyze why your delegation failed."

Explain the task. "Recall a time when you delegated work that was not subsequently performed. Write three reasons that this might have occurred."

Give an example. "For instance, I once assigned an employee a priority report to be completed in a week. . . . The third reason may have been that the employee was relatively new and felt insecure about doing a good job."

Specify the context. "Take five minutes to do this individually."

Explain what is to be reported. "Be ready to share your incident, as well as the potential reasons for it, with the total group."

Option. Restate the instructions in shorthand. "It's important to think through your actions before you take them. Recall a delegation that failed, and write three possible reasons. Take five minutes working alone, and be ready to share your incident and reasons."

Figure 5-8. Sample of Instructions Plus an Example

In Chapter 4, Making Presentations, it was mentioned that the biggest problem trainers have in using handouts is giving them to the learners too soon. Consequently, it was suggested that handouts not be distributed while you are talking because learners may read them instead of listening. The same suggestion applies here, with one exception: A handout can be distributed if you tell the learners to follow along as it is read aloud. This procedure allows you to keep the learners' attention as you emphasize certain points.

Give the introduction/rationale. "Interviewing is a vital but difficult skill that all managers need. To improve your skill in this important area, you will now have a chance to practice the techniques presented."

Explain the task. "You are about to role play an interview with a problem employee. After the role play, you will receive an evaluation of your performance."

Specify the context. "Using the prepared role play that I'm going to distribute, you are to work in groups of three with people you know the least well. In each subgroup each member will have the opportunity to play the roles of interviewer, person being interviewed, and observer. Each role play should last about ten minutes. The observer is in charge of keeping time and managing the evaluation. After each role play, the person playing the interviewer will speak first, evaluating his or her own performance. Then the person playing the role of the one interviewed will provide feedback to the interviewer, using the observation sheet that you'll find on your table."

Explain what is to be reported. "When everyone is finished, be prepared to report your reactions to the experience, particularly what you found most difficult."

Distribute the handouts. "The handout I'm distributing now describes the roles and summarizes the procedures I just explained. After you've formed your groups, you can review it if you need help in getting started."

Figure 5-9. Sample of Instructions Plus a Handout

SUMMARY

Giving clear, precise instructions in a guiding rather than controlling way is one of the most difficult tasks for trainers. Studying the figures in this chapter and practicing repeatedly will help to make the process of giving instructions simpler for you, more informative for the learners, and more effective in accomplishing the learning goals of the training program.

You are urged to follow the four-step guide presented in this chapter. The cardinal principle to remember is to give the rationale for the activity before describing the task, how it is to be done, and what will be reported. We believe that this procedure is the closest thing to a "sure-fire" formula for helping learners to participate more productively in the activities of a training program and to draw the greatest learning from them.

Chapter 6
Monitoring Individual and Subgroup Tasks

After you have given task instructions, you must monitor the learners' work. In this case, monitoring means keeping track of certain signals or cues, not directing or supervising the learners' work.

There are two main reasons for monitoring learners' work. The first is that it gives you the information needed to ascertain whether the learners are on target and proceeding appropriately. If you sense confusion or misinterpretation, the task needs to be restated, either in shorthand or with the addition of an example.

The second reason for monitoring is to determine whether and how to adjust the time needed for the task. Even the best design may need adjustments in the time scheduled for certain activities. Your focus should be on what amount of time produces the best learning. Tasks are not timed with a stopwatch.

STAY IN THE ROOM

Avoid the inclination to walk away or to return to your notes after giving the instructions for a task. Instead, stand quietly and wait for the learners to begin their work. Attention should be given to the learners until they are settled down and working. At that point you can relax and begin to prepare for the next activity, although you should still monitor what is happening occasionally.

It is best not to walk out of the room unless absolutely necessary. Your presence may be needed to clarify or to provide assistance.

DO NOT INTRUDE

Stay in the room, but do not intrude on the learners while they are working. Most trainers tend to want to "help." Sometimes they are tempted to approach learners or subgroups and ask, "How are you doing?" In order to answer, learners must interrupt their efforts and risk losing their train of thought or their momentum. Intruding in this way may satisfy your curiosity or make you feel more useful, but it stops the learning process. Sometimes when the trainer stands close to a subgroup without saying anything, learners think it is necessary to include the trainer, so they will politely make room or ask a question. This trainer behavior is another way of taking learners away from their task. It is better for the trainer to keep his or her distance and allow the learners to do their work. At the beginning simply watch from the front of the room; then, as work progresses, feel free to move around if desired, but without being obtrusive.

WHEN TO INTERVENE

Occasionally, after giving instructions, you will find that at least one subgroup has not really understood them. When this is true, you need to intervene and offer some help. If you feel that the instructions have been explained adequately in general and only one subgroup misunderstood them, the members of that subgroup should be helped to understand what it is they are to do; after clarifying the assignment, you can leave the subgroup to its work.

However, if you think that other subgroups also may have misunderstood, you can interrupt all subgroups and restate the task for everyone. It is probably not necessary to repeat all four steps of the instructions in such a situation, but certainly it is necessary to repeat the explanation of the task and perhaps what is to be reported. When there is confusion, it is usually for one of the following reasons:

- The task itself is not clear;
- The four-step process for giving instructions was not followed;
- What you said about the task was misunderstood;

- The task is perceived as inappropriate; or
- One member of a subgroup is distracting the others from the task.

The last two situations are very rare. It is not necessary to identify the specific problem at the moment at which the confusion takes place. Just restating the instructions is usually sufficient to allow the learners to begin their work.

CUES TO WATCH FOR

Subgroup Formation

It is part of your monitoring responsibility to be aware of how the learners are forming their subgroups and to help them rearrange if necessary in a way that is more conducive to their learning. For example, Figure 6-1 illustrates some subgroup configurations that are detrimental to learning. In this figure the arrows indicate the direction of the interaction. When one of these types of configurations occurs, you need to intervene and make adjustments so that the resulting configuration looks something like that shown in Figure 6-2.

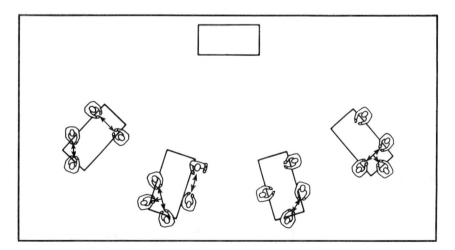

Figure 6-1. Subgroup Configurations That Are Detrimental to Learning

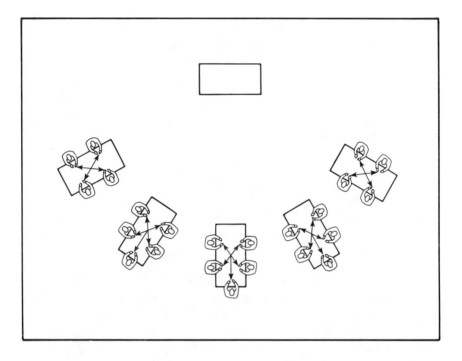

Figure 6-2. Subgroup Configuration That Is Conducive to Learning

Noise Level

Listen to the noise level in the room and notice when it goes up or down. A change in the noise level indicates that something in the room has changed. For example, it may mean either that learners are working harder or that they have completed their task.

Verbal Cues

Listen carefully to catch words and phrases. This kind of aural scanning is just as important as the visual checks that you make while the subgroups are working. For example, if you hear words like "appraisal," "communication," or "interview" during an exercise on performance appraisal, you can assume that the members of that particular subgroup are working on the task. If, on the other hand, you hear learners discussing unrelated matters, you will know that they have either completed the task or avoided it. Picking up on random words and phrases can give you a clue as to the learners' progress in their work.

Nonverbal Cues

We do not believe that isolated gestures are particularly good indicators of feelings or reactions, but we do believe that total body position is. For example, when people are intensely involved in something, they look intent. Similarly, it is easy to tell when people are relaxed and talking casually; legs may be crossed and arms may be resting on the backs of chairs, for example. Look for these broad indicators rather than for specific, individual positions or gestures.

Time

You need to be watchful of the time. In Chapter 5, Giving Instructions, it was noted that the amount of time assigned for a task guides subgroup members toward completion of that task. It is important for you to help the learners monitor their use of time. If it happens that the prescribed period of time has passed and people are still working intently, with valuable learning taking place, allow their work to continue.

When some people or subgroups have finished and others have not, it is helpful to announce a time check by saying something like "There are about two more minutes left." In this case announce whatever amount of time you think it will take those who have finished to review and those who have not finished to speed up and complete the task. This technique influences the slower individuals or groups to complete their work, while reassuring those who have finished that they did so within reasonable time constraints.

MONITORING HANDS-ON COMPUTER ACTIVITIES

Presenting information, giving instructions, and managing the sharing process are no different when the learners are involved in computer training. The process of monitoring, however, is very different. To enhance the learning potential, keep the following tips in mind:

Do not touch a learner's computer. Some trainers have a tendency to reach over the shoulder of a learner and to show him or her what to do. This tendency should be avoided. Reaching over someone's shoulder is an infringement and is more likely to interrupt learning than to facilitate it.

Explain the work purpose of any activity before explaining which keys to press or what procedure to use. Learners need to understand what the objective is before they can be expected to employ particular procedures to achieve the desired results. In other words they need to know where they are going before they begin. When learners understand the reason for a certain approach, they are better able to relate procedures to applications.

Avoid patronizing remarks. Some "user-friendly" computer programs are designed to respond to the learner in a way that can be perceived as patronizing. For example, one program asks the learner to type in his or her name and then responds by saying, "That's good, John. You typed your name in as directed." If at all possible, avoid such programs, and certainly avoid using patronizing language. There is a difference between offering a patronizing remark and making encouraging statements.

Train the person; do not teach the material. Be aware of each individual person in the room—his or her abilities, successes, problems, and frustrations. Treat each one individually. Focus on responding to the learners, not on covering the material. Although a strong focus on covering the material sometimes gives the illusion of competence, a truly competent trainer sees his or her job as that of assisting people in learning.

Train people to think, not just to do or to follow instructions. Be sure that they understand the work-related reasons for everything they do before they are asked to do it.

Avoid the overuse of jargon. Use technical terms sparingly, and use only those that the learners need to learn. Do not "show off" by using jargon. A true expert does not have to rely on technical terms, but can explain in such a way that the nontechnical learner can understand.

Be patient. The learners may suffer from frustration and express it, and that is perfectly acceptable. However, keep your own frustration under control. Patience pays off in terms of helping people to learn.

Do not let people fall behind. Many computer courses are like foreign-language courses. Those who have the most difficulty may fall behind. Because all future learning is dependent on past and present knowledge, even one episode of falling behind can cause a person to become so lost that he or she eventually "drops out"—mentally, emotionally, or literally.

Keep the more experienced people busy. Be sure to have enough material for activities so that additional tasks can be assigned to those who are proficient and complete their work early. Be careful, however, not to assign "busy work"; any additional task assigned should be more complex than the one just completed so that the advanced learners remain challenged and, therefore, increase their learning.

Use the process of leading questions. Sometimes referred to as the "Socratic method," this process calls for asking a series of leading questions that help learners discover the proper sequence of action and, hence, arrive at the proper answer. This procedure is *inappropriate* in training that does not involve hands-on computer work, where it can be seen as disrespectful, patronizing, and manipulative; it often causes people to tune out or, in some cases, to rebel openly. On the other hand, the use of this process in computer training is entirely *appropriate* because it helps learners to think in a way that enables them to understand how a computer works and how to take charge of and manipulate the computer. The Socratic method is not easy to use, but skill in employing it can be developed with practice. It requires a trainer to do the following:

- Identify the problem that the learner is facing;
- Determine the proper sequence of action that will help the learner to solve the problem; and

- Ask a series of questions that will help the learner to discover the predetermined proper sequence.

When a learner is having a problem, you can do one of four things:

- Ignore the situation, thereby forcing the learner to figure out the solution to the problem;
- Use the process of leading questions, thereby helping the learner to discover the proper sequence of action;
- Tell the learner what to do and why it should be done; or
- Take over for the learner and use the keyboard to solve the problem.

Each of these approaches is appropriate at different times. For example, it is appropriate to ignore a learner when he or she is overly dependent and has the ability to solve the problem. It is also appropriate to use leading questions when it is important that the learner think through the issues. Similarly, it is appropriate to tell the learner what to do when doing so will facilitate learning and will not waste the learner's problem-solving skills. Occasionally it is even appropriate to take over. For example, if a learner has accidentally called up something on the computer that is totally unrelated to the present activity, you may want to take over and manipulate the computer to return it to the appropriate place or menu. Whichever method is used, be aware of the reasons for using that particular method and the potential impact on the learner.

Chapter 7
Managing the Reporting Process

The last part of a learning activity is usually some kind of reporting process. Learners exchange with one another the discoveries made and insights reached during their task work. Occasionally the training design requires individuals to report on what they learned while working alone; but, more often than not, reporting refers to the exchange of subgroup learnings, usually by means of oral reports from subgroup representatives.

The term _reporting process_ does not refer to a blow-by-blow account of the work done by each subgroup. That sort of recitation can be redundant and tedious and can inhibit the learning process. Instead, the word "report" refers to a disclosure or revelation of what each subgroup learned. This part of a training program should provide an extension of the learning that everyone enjoyed, not simply a statement of the learners' approach to a particular task.

The emphasis on the reporting process will vary with the nature of the tasks or exercises in the training program. With some tasks the potential learning lies exclusively in doing the activity. This is often true of individual-reflection exercises. Discussion afterward would not add anything and might detract. In these cases, therefore, the design will not call for sharing reports. Sometimes the greatest learning is experienced during the reporting process itself, rather than in the activity preceding it. For example, in human relations training, a short role play may be followed by extensive "processing" in which learners reach many new insights and understandings. Here, the training design should allow more time for sharing the learners' reports. Most frequently, learning occurs both in doing the activity and in the report sharing afterward.

In delivering training be aware of the significance of the reporting process to people's learning. Sometimes, when subgroup work runs over the allotted time, it is tempting to catch up by cutting short the reports. Instead, try to make several small adjustments or, if possible, end the reporting process at a later time than anticipated. Most packaged programs specify the amount of time needed for the reporting process, and they frequently designate particular methods to accomplish the intended learning goals.

After the subgroups have completed their work, review what will be reported and explain *how* it will be reported. The content of the reports already will have been defined in the earlier instructions, and presumably each subgroup is prepared; but it is at this point that you inform the learners of the format for the reporting process. This involves three main steps: reassembling the total group, requesting the reports, and synthesizing or adding to the reports.

REASSEMBLING THE TOTAL GROUP

As mentioned earlier, it is a good idea to announce a time check when the learners have almost completed their work. They should be told approximately how much time they have before they will reassemble as a total group, and this should be done in facilitating language such as "It's time to meet together" or "Let's hear what each subgroup has to say." This kind of comment helps the learners to make the transition from a subgroup activity to a total-group reporting session. On the other hand, controlling language, such as "You must report now" or "You have used all the time I have given you," is much less effective.

There are many ways to help learners to complete their work. If all subgroups are ready but one, you might stand next to that subgroup's table, for example. If this subtle approach does not work, you can ask a question such as "How much time do you need?" or "Can you report in the next few moments?" If there are scattered subgroups or individuals still working, you can stand in front of the room, awaiting the completion of all the subgroups' work and their attention. In some situations, particularly in very large rooms, you may have to project your voice to reconvene the total group.

It is a good idea to try several ways of helping people to complete their work and rejoin the total group. Eventually you will find which ways work best for you. Be careful to use only those techniques that are facilitating and that demonstrate respect for the learners, as opposed to those that are teacher oriented and controlling.

FOUR WAYS TO REQUEST REPORTS

Once the total group has been reassembled, it is your job to specify how the learning will be shared. This choice is based on three factors: the learning activity involved, the learning goals, and the need to vary the procedure. There are four common ways in which to request reports. At first the variety of options available in managing the reporting process may seem confusing. But as you gain experience and familiarity with them, managing the reports will become easy, comfortable, and enjoyable for both you and the learners. Your skill in using different kinds of reporting methods provides a change of pace for the learners and adds rhythmic variety to the training program.

1. Subgroup Samples

Requesting subgroup samples is a way of obtaining a little information from each subgroup so that the sum of the reports equals the total product for the task. It is generally used when the subgroups have been asked to compile the same kind of list. This method allows each subgroup an opportunity to make a report of approximately the same length. Figure 7-1 is an example of how to request reports in the form of subgroup samples.

Task instructions. "Identify and list the most important qualities of a competent salesperson."

Request for reports. "Let's hear a couple of qualities that each subgroup identified."

Figure 7-1. Requesting Subgroup Samples

2. One Complete Report Plus Additions

Another method of requesting reports is to ask one subgroup to begin by making a complete report and the other subgroups to follow with contributions of additional information. This method is best used when the subgroups have been given different assignments. The learning takes place both during the performance of the assigned tasks and while the learners are listening to the reports of others. Figure 7-2 presents an example of how to request reports in this fashion.

Task instructions. "We have examined the purposes for holding different types of meetings, each requiring a different procedure and style of leadership. So that you can practice with these types, each group will examine a different type of meeting and list the ideal procedure as well as describe the leader's role and activities. Group 1, you will examine a staff meeting; Group 2, a sales meeting; Group 3, a problem-solving meeting involving conflict between two divisions; and Group 4, a planning or goal-setting meeting."

Request for reports. "Group 1, what procedures did you identify for the staff meeting, and what leadership role and activities did you describe?" After the report delivered by Group 1, the trainer asks, "Group 2, what questions and comments can you add?" After the additional information offered by Group 2, the trainer repeats the process of requesting additional questions and comments from each subgroup until all have shared the results of their investigations.

Figure 7-2. Requesting One Complete Report Plus Additions

3. Formal Presentations

This method involves asking a representative from each subgroup to make a presentation of the issue that the subgroup investigated and its resolution to that issue. Formal presentations are most effective when the subgroups have been assigned different tasks or have been asked to take a slightly different approach to some aspect of the same task. The advantage of this method is that it allows each subgroup to learn from investigating a complete problem or issue as well as from hearing presentations about different experiences involving the investigation of other subjects or issues. Figure 7-3 presents an example of how to request formal presentations.

Task instructions. "Pretend that you have just assumed the role of managing the data-processing function in a medium-sized company. You have been asked to prepare a long-range development plan for the data-processing function. What kind of information might you seek and why? Group 1, your task is to gather information from top management; Group 2, from your staff; and Group 3, from the managers below your level in the company. Each group is to take fifteen minutes to prepare its list of information, and each group is to appoint one person to report the list."

Request for reports. "Group 1, you focused on top management. Tell us what information you would seek and why." After the report, the information is evaluated and discussed by the total group; then the trainer says, "Group 2, you sought information from your staff. What would you seek and why?" Again the information provided in the report is evaluated and discussed, and then the trainer repeats this process for Group 3.

Figure 7-3. Requesting Formal Presentations

4. Polling

Polling is a technique in which all the subgroups are asked to respond quickly with their answers to a proposed problem. You do not comment on any subgroup's answer until all subgroups have been polled. Polling is best used when the end product of a task is a single answer, such as a number or a yes/no decision. The advantage of this method is that it can bring synthesis and closure to an exercise in which most of the work and learning have occurred in the subgroups. It also allows for a rich, cross-group discussion when differing answers are given. Figure 7-4 provides an example of how to poll.

Task instructions. "This task will help you to gain skill in selecting the right candidate for a job. You are about to examine a job description for branch manager and several resumes. After reading this material, reach a consensus in your subgroup on which person you would recommend for the job."

Request for reports. "Group 1, which candidate would you recommend?" After receiving the response, the trainer asks each subgroup the same question. After all answers have been received, each subgroup is asked to explain why it recommended a particular person. The trainer then provides synthesis by stating the principles underlying the subgroup decisions.

Figure 7-4. Polling

LOGISTICAL DETAILS

Selection of Subgroup Spokespersons

One detail that must be considered as part of the reporting process is the selection of subgroup spokespersons. Spokespersons are almost always needed. You may explicitly instruct each subgroup to appoint a spokesperson in advance, or the subgroups may be allowed to decide on their own who will report when the time comes. Once the learners have had some experience with discovery learning, it seems natural and normal to them to share the responsibility of reporting. However, the first time a subgroup is asked to report, there may be some reluctance, so it is best to ask the members to appoint someone ahead of time. Subsequently, when the subgroups become familiar with the procedures, you need not be so explicit.

Time

Another detail is the question of time. The reporting methods described in this chapter help learners to review and extend their learning in varying degrees of depth and completeness. Therefore, they require varying amounts of time. When adjustments must be made in the program schedule, the method of reporting is one thing that can be altered easily.

One way to do this is to limit or restrict the reports in some way, as is done when requesting subgroup samples. For example, when subgroups are making formal presentations, you may ask each subgroup to mention the "two most important" points that were discovered.

Another way is to substitute a method that usually requires less time. If twenty learners are working in four groups of five each, the reporting process using any given method will take the same amount of time as for sixteen learners in four groups of four each. Rule-of-thumb estimates of the length of time required for reports from four groups, by method, are as follows:

- Subgroup samples: ten to twenty minutes;
- One complete report plus additions: fifteen to twenty-five minutes;
- Formal presentations: twenty to thirty minutes; and
- Polling: five to fifteen minutes.

This should provide an idea of the time adjustments possible with each reporting method. You should keep in mind that the purpose and results of each method are different; therefore, it is not advisable to substitute randomly a different method just to save time. However, be knowledgeable about and in command of all possible variations in a program as it is being delivered.

Props

The last logistical detail that needs to be considered is the issue of props as reporting tools. Sometimes trainers feel that they have to write down what learners say in order to acknowledge their reports. We recommend that you acknowledge them verbally and that transparencies or newsprint be used only when it is necessary to emphasize some point, to save the information for later, or to keep all the items visible for the purpose of synthesis or review. An example of the latter would be using newsprint to organize the reports. If each subgroup names some advantages and disadvantages, for example, you might want to list them on two separate sheets of newsprint.

SKILLS NEEDED TO MANAGE
THE REPORTING PROCESS

Managing the reporting process effectively requires the following basic skills:

- Asking initiating and clarifying questions;
- Paraphrasing;
- Summarizing;
- Extending; and
- Using nonverbal cues.

It is not easy to convey the subtle way in which these skills contribute to the effectiveness of the process, and there are few rules about what one can and cannot do. The following tips are merely guidelines on how to help learners to exchange and extend their learnings.

Initiating and Clarifying Questions

To help initiate and encourage full reports, you need to be able to ask direct, but not leading, questions. It is best to ask open-ended questions, usually beginning with what, when, where, or how. It is usually best not to use "why" questions because they tend to be viewed as "attacking" or "confronting." It is better to use requesting language, such as "Describe your reasons for choosing that approach" or "Tell us the factors that led to that decision." The following are some more examples of open-ended questions and probes:

- "What was the most challenging part of the task?"
- "How did your group approach the problem?"
- "Describe what makes this technique important."
- "What are your remaining questions?"

When you use open-ended questions or probes, the responses are quite different from those received when closed-ended questions are asked. Usually a closed-ended question can be answered with "yes" or "no." The following are some examples of closed-ended questions:

- "Was the task challenging for your group?"
- "Do you want to tell us what you came up with?"
- "Is this technique important?"
- "Do you have any more questions?"

Another kind of question that does not work well is one that has an open-ended intent but a closed format. Examples are "Does anyone know?" or "Can anyone tell us the implications for the job?" Such questions are basically unanswerable unless you take a poll.

Paraphrasing

The goal of paraphrasing is to demonstrate that you are listening and understanding what is being reported. Learners appreciate knowing that they have been heard accurately.

There are four types of paraphrasing:

1. *Restatement.* You state, in your own words rather than the learner's, a condensed version of what has just been said. (Restating in the learner's words is simply parroting; it communicates that you *heard* the learner statement, but not that you *understood* it.)

2. *General to specific.* If the learner statement involved is general, you paraphrase it by stating a specific part of the statement or an example. By stating the specific, you show that you understood the general.

3. *Specific to general.* If the learner statement is specific, you paraphrase by stating a generalization or principle. By formulating a broader response, you indicate not only that you understood the learner's statement, but also that the learner's statement can, in fact, be generalized.

4. *Restatement in opposite terms.* You convey that you understood the meaning of the learner statement by restating it in terms that are opposite to those used by the learner. For example, if the learner says that a manager *should* do something, you could restate the learner comment by saying that the manager should *not* do the opposite.

Consider the following learner statement: "Auditing really requires the auditor to have a special kind of cautious optimism." You might paraphrase this statement in any of the following ways:

- *Restatement:* "You mean that the auditor should be open but still careful."
- *General to specific:* "An auditor should carefully check every entry."
- *Specific to general:* "Sounds as though you think auditing is complex."
- *Restatement in opposite terms:* "You're saying that the auditor should not be negative and overly suspicious."

Paraphrasing encourages learners to say more because they know that they have been understood. One important point to remember is to look for a sign that the learner agrees with the paraphrasing. If no sign is given, either verbal or nonverbal, ask the learner whether the statement has been paraphrased accurately. If you make mistakes without checking, then you are demonstrating misunderstanding, which will have exactly the opposite effect on the learning climate from that intended when paraphrasing.

Summarizing

Summarizing is a technique that is similar to paraphrasing, but with a slight difference. The goal of paraphrasing is to *mirror the meaning* to check for understanding, whereas the goal of summarizing is to *synthesize* to check for understanding. You synthesize by condensing the meaning of the learner's comments into a sentence or two (or, if the comments were lengthy, into a paragraph) and repeating the synthesized information as a summary.

Summarizing typically begins with such phrases as the following:

- "In other words, . . .";
- "What you're saying is that. . ."; and
- "In summary, you think that. . . ."

You need to be careful about the use of certain phrases when summarizing. For example, too many uses of a phrase such as "What I hear that you're saying" to introduce summaries can begin to sound mechanical and condescending.

Extending

The purpose of extending is to add scope or depth to a learner's comments. If the addition matches the spirit of the initial statement, it not only communicates understanding but also enriches. Either *technical information* or *information about personal feelings* can be extended.

Technical information refers to that which a learner reports after completing a task. In this case you add to the report with additional data: "You make a good point about the auditor's role in analyzing the financial statement of a corporation. In addition, the auditor needs to ensure that all current regulations are met."

Information about personal feelings refers to that which a learner offers about himself or herself during the course of a training session. You can add to this kind of information, but you must be very careful in doing so. Extending in this way requires you to empathize strongly with the learner. It is a very powerful method for demonstrating deep understanding, but it is also quite difficult to do convincingly and effectively. Here are two examples of what a trainer might say when extending personal information:

- "So you advised your boss to sue. I was once in exactly the same position. I supervised the EEO function of personnel, and...."
- "I agree. After I recovered from the initial shock of my father's death, I felt lonely and angry as well."

Using Gestures, Movement, and Body Stance During Reporting

Your nonverbal behavior can communicate understanding and can help contribute to a positive learning environment during the reporting process. Certain nonverbal behaviors also can have a detrimental effect: If you shake your head in disapproval, roll your eyes to the ceiling, frown, or suddenly put your hands on your hips, you may convey a negative judgment to a learner and reduce the risks that the learner may take during the training.

It is appropriate for you to nod your head to indicate understanding or to encourage further participation. It is also acceptable to say "uh-huh" for the same purpose. However, you should not overdo either of these behaviors. Repeated use of them can be seen as manipulative rather than as an honest desire to listen and encourage.

Use gestures and body positioning in a way that says you are simply facilitating the sharing among learners. This may take some practice. When a subgroup is reporting, for example, it is natural to walk toward its members in order to hear them better. This is particularly true when the spokesperson speaks softly. However, it is best to stand at some distance to encourage the person to speak up. Moving away may not come naturally, but try to remember to do it. All of the learners will be able to hear better and will feel more involved in the report.

MAINTAINING AUTHENTICITY

A discussion of the interpersonal skills needed to manage the reporting process would be incomplete without readdressing the issue of authenticity. When paraphrasing, extending, or demonstrating understanding through the use of nonverbal behaviors, you must be authentic rather than manipulative or artificial.

The reporting process is an opportunity for the learners to enhance their learning, not for the trainer to teach. Stay out of the way as much as possible, trying not to dominate the discussion and trying not to feel that all comments must be directed to or through you. Instead, learners should be encouraged to talk to one another. You do not need to comment on everything that is said. Sometimes a simple "thank you" is best. In addition, avoid expressing agreement or disagreement with any learner comment; your opinion may not be relevant or helpful.

In summary, we offer the following tips for facilitating the reporting process:

- Do not teach.
- Do not control learners so that they answer or behave the way you think they should.
- Say "I don't know" when you do not know.
- Allow disagreement.
- Create a warm, encouraging climate.
- Be aware of the learning that is taking place.

Chapter 8

____Managing Learning Activities____

Adult learning designs are generally dependent on one or more of five methods: presentation, group discussion, simulation, skill practice, and nonverbal techniques. These five methods are addressed in this chapter. To give you a better feel for "andragogy in action," we offer some pointers to keep in mind when using each of these methods.

PRESENTATION METHODS

Presentation methods are used generally when knowledge acquisition is the learning goal. Lectures, demonstrations, and audiovisual presentations are examples, as are panel discussions, debates, and interviews. With any presentation method, your main concern is helping learners to obtain new information, internalize new concepts, and experience new ideas.

Five Traps for Trainers

The art and skill of making presentations is discussed in Chapter 4, which concentrates on the short presentations that are usually incorporated into discovery-learning designs. The trainer who has mastered the techniques suggested in that chapter can, with a bit of forethought and perhaps some practice, easily adapt them to other situations. Whatever you do, you should strive to avoid the five traps into which a trainer may fall when using presentation methods:

"I got through the material." Covering the training material does not necessarily result in learning. You may be familiar with the legendary definition of a college lecture: a process whereby the notes on the pad of the professor are transferred to the pad of the student without going through the head of either. Pay attention to the learners' reactions to the presentation by continually scanning the room and by asking direct questions; it is only in this way that you can determine whether the information being presented is understandable, relevant, and useful to the audience.

"They seemed to like it." Another trap to avoid is the desire to be entertaining. There is nothing wrong with having fun in a training session. But when you try to be entertaining, you risk a situation in which the learners are amused rather than gain satisfaction from their learning. Learning should be *enjoyable* rather than *amusing.*

The biggest problem with trying to be entertaining is that you may never know whether your efforts have resulted in useful learning. When you are entertaining without facilitating learning, you may receive a number of compliments from learners, such as "I really enjoyed your presentation" or "I'm going to attend every session you do from now on." If you hear this kind of remark very often, you should examine the situation carefully to determine to what extent you are entertaining at the expense of helping people to learn.

"I'm the expert." Regardless of whether you are an expert, you should not act like one. You are more knowledgeable about the subject matter dealt with in the training than are the learners; however, this knowledge does not make you "smarter." The learners are adults with their own experiences, attitudes, and judgment faculties. You must not act as though you have "the answer." Instead, your job is to help learners to discover the relevance of the program's learning opportunities to their own work and lives.

"I'm so important." You are a person with some interesting ideas, but so is every learner in the training session. Your ideas may be a bit better organized with regard to some subjects, but you should remember that it is easier for people to listen to and accept new ideas when they are presented with an *authoritative* attitude rather than a *superior* one.

"I delivered the speech perfectly." The trainer falls into this trap when he or she follows the presentation outline in a mechanical way. No speech stands alone. The best presentations are given with appropriate enthusiasm, dedication, integrity, concern, and a heavy dose of the trainer's own special personality.

Reminders

You should not only know the material; you should believe it and "own" it. Every presentation should be delivered in your own words and style. This means that you must take the time to assimilate the content and to practice presenting it until it flows naturally and easily. Presentation skills should be fine-tuned until they are almost second nature.

In addition, strive to be in tune with the learners in mind, spirit, and body. This means paying attention to their reactions, letting them know that they are valued as people, and being physically and psychologically accessible rather than hiding behind an imposing podium or being preoccupied with training gadgets and tricks.

QUESTION-AND-ANSWER PERIODS

Many training designs call for a question-and-answer period after a presentation. Too often a trainer asks the group, "Are there any questions?" Sometimes the responses are useful and provocative questions or comments, and sometimes there is a long silence followed by a question from a learner who is speaking up only to rescue the situation. On other occasions learner reactions may include speeches phrased as questions, or silence followed by more silence. You can never be sure that a question-and-answer period will be useful or productive. An absence of reaction to a call for questions may or may not mean that the presentation was right on target and that the learners are ready to proceed with the next phase of the learning design.

We have found a technique that works very well in generating relevant, useful questions without seeming to control them: using the subgroup process for the purpose of formulating questions. The main advantage of this technique is that it yields a workable number of questions and issues that the learners wish to have explained or expanded. Another advantage is that the trainer can avoid being presented with an irrelevant question or trapped into entering a discussion with someone who has a special ax to grind.

After the presentation the trainer asks the learners to assemble into subgroups to formulate those questions that they think others would find most interesting. Instructions should be given as clearly and carefully as they would for any other subgroup task, using the four steps described in Chapter 5. Figure 8-1 presents sample instructions for subgroups.

"I have finished the formal part of my presentation. I hope it has raised some questions for you. It's important that the information presented be relevant and helpful to you in your work.

"So that our discussion of the presentation will be as relevant as possible, I'd like you to get together with two or three other people sitting near you and spend five minutes sharing your reactions to the presentation and determining among yourselves what questions you would like me to respond to. Focus on the questions that are important to you and that you think would interest others in this training session. Move your chairs in any way you wish so that you can assemble into groups more easily.

"Appoint one person in your group to jot down the questions generated and to share them when your group is asked for its input. I will answer as many as I can. Please begin."

**Figure 8-1. Sample Instructions to Subgroups
to Generate Questions**

When the trainer has finished giving instructions, task-monitoring skills should come into play. People who have been sitting and listening often need some encouragement to switch from a passive to a more active mode. There are a number of things that you can do to help the question-generating process to work:

- Expect learners to follow instructions. You often get what you expect.
- Tell the learners that although they did not anticipate this task, the questions generated in this way will be helpful to everyone.
- Make eye contact and use nonverbal behaviors to communicate the importance of the learners' talking together in subgroups.
- Repeat the instructions in shorthand before asking the learners to begin.

After the allotted time (generally just a few minutes), call the learners together and use the techniques discussed in Chapter 7 that pertain to asking for and responding to questions.

If the total group consists of only ten to twenty learners, you may ask each subgroup for its most important question first (a variation of the subgroup-samples approach; see Chapter 7, page 85). If the total group consists of thirty-five or more learners, you may ask for questions from subgroups in different sections of the room. It is often a good idea to start with a statement such as this: "I'd like to hear four or five questions now. After I've heard them, I'll respond. Then, if there's still time, I'll ask for other questions. Group 2, let's hear one question that was raised during your discussion."

Regardless of how you decide to conduct a question-and-answer period, it is usually a good idea to take several questions from learners before the answering process begins. Although this approach may feel awkward at first, we think that it offers important advantages by allowing you to do the following:

- Respond to the most important questions first;
- Link the answers to several questions together;
- Control the time better; and
- Avoid being trapped into answering irrelevant or "special-interest" questions.

SUBGROUP-DISCUSSION ACTIVITIES

Subgroup-discussion activities, such as problem-solving exercises and case-study evaluations, are methods that are commonly used when the learning goal is understanding. These kinds of activities require learners to use their knowledge and experience as well as their skills in analysis, decision making, and creative thinking to gain new understanding or insight regarding a particular concept or idea.

In problem-solving exercises learners are usually asked to "solve" a problem by answering the question "What would you do and why?" In case evaluations learners analyze a written case, usually to answer the question "What went wrong and why?" Subgroup-discussion activities are typically designed to draw some "product" from the learners' knowledge and experience—for example, a list of the advantages and disadvantages in taking the tell-and-sell approach to interviewing job applicants or a list of the reasons that a salesperson might follow a particular sequence of actions in handling a customer complaint.

The situations posed to learners in problem-solving exercises, case analyses, and other subgroup-discussion activities should be "reality based," that is, similar or analogous, if not identical, to situations that the learners face in their work or in their lives. Generally, these tasks are so straightforward that they do not require any extraordinary delivery skills. The following material is a review of important points to keep in mind when using a subgroup-discussion activity:

Make sure that the learners see the activity as potentially useful to them and worth doing. Do not belittle the value of the activity by introducing it as "a little exercise." If the activity is worth doing, treat it as such so that the learners will do the same.

Do not distribute handouts or materials for the task until the instructions have been given. When learners receive a handout, they frequently are tempted to begin reading it at the expense of hearing what they need to know about doing the task.

Allow learners enough time to become intellectually and emotionally involved. Do not shorten the time specified in the design. Much of the learning takes place in the subgroup discussion on which such an activity is based; therefore, ensure that the time allotted for this discussion is adequate.

Be careful not to dominate the task with your own personal views. The overriding purpose of a subgroup-discussion activity is to provide an opportunity for learners to gain understanding—not facts, opinions, or basic knowledge. Encourage divergent thinking, lively discussion, different points of view, and creative approaches. Let the learners explore different answers or solutions.

SIMULATION ACTIVITIES

Structured experiences and role plays involving such things as in-basket exercises, case studies, and critical incidents are some of the so-called "simulation methods" aimed at increasing understanding, developing skills, even changing attitudes and values. They frequently appear in programs designed to develop interpersonal skills that will help learners to increase their competence in managing their working and personal relationships.

In management training, simulation methods are often used to help people to improve their skills in delegating work, giving and receiving feedback, interviewing, and working as part of a project team. In sales training, simulation methods help people to learn face-to-face selling skills, such as establishing rapport with the customer, making the sales presentation, overcoming objections, and closing the sale. Simulation methods also are used in training programs designed to develop cognitive or knowledge skills, such as analytical and creative thinking, decision making, synthesis, and problem solving. Most simulation methods require the use of small subgroups or pairs. Some of them—case studies, in-basket exercises, and critical incidents, for example—are suitable for individual work.

Structured Experiences

Structured experiences[2] involve learners in an activity seemingly
unrelated to their real lives, on the job or off. Unless the structured
experience includes a role play, the learners are essentially instructed
to "be themselves" and "to act naturally" in responding to some situation that is outside the realm of their knowledge or practical experience.
Usually the purpose is to stimulate insight into individual or group
behavior; that insight is then generalized and applied to the real world.
In addition, some structured experiences incorporate an element of
potential competition among the participating groups.

Most designs for structured experiences call for the following
sequence of events:

1. The trainer introduces and explains the activity, stating any
   "rules" or other stipulations that apply.
2. The learners complete the activity.
4. The learners analyze what they experienced during the activity.
5. The learners apply their analysis of the experience to the real
   world.

Following certain guidelines with regard to presenting, giving task
instructions, monitoring, and managing the reporting process can help
the trainer to successfully implement the four-step procedure when using
structured experiences.

---

[2]Training literature is full of structured experiences. University
Associates has published several hundred in its *Handbook* and *Annual* series;
some of the more widely known of these include "Lost at Sea," "Hampshire
In-Basket," "Hollow Square," "One-Way, Two-Way," and "Prisoners' Dilem-
ma." Teleometrics International has published the well-known structured
experiences "NASA Exercise," "Lost on the Moon," and "Moon Survival."
"Desert Survival," another popular structured experience, is distributed by
Human Synergistics. Refer to the Resources appendix for these and other
sources of structured experiences.

Presenting

Effective learning from structured experiences rarely depends on any kind of "content input" beforehand. If the design calls for a presentation as part of the introduction to the activity, it should be short and to the point.

Giving Task Instructions

When delivering the introduction and providing task instructions, you must explain why the activity is potentially useful to the learners. If a rationale does not appear in the guidelines for conducting the activity, you should build one into the design. After the rationale has been presented, you should ensure that the learners have understood and accepted it.

Most published structured experiences have precise instructions. If a structured experience stipulates reading the instructions verbatim to the learners, you should do so. If such a stipulation is not included, instructions should be written beforehand and then read to the learners. Precision and clarity are critical in giving instructions.

Newsprint, transparencies, or handouts should be used to summarize any rules, the time allotted, and other facts that learners need to know, particularly if the activity is lengthy or complex. In addition, the learners should be told whether the rules are subject to change during the activity. Finally, it is a good idea to check at least twice to make sure that the rules and procedures are clear to the learners before they begin the activity.

Monitoring

Be accessible and helpful, but stay out of the way. It is not acceptable to participate in what the subgroups are doing, but it is essential to keep track of what is happening within the subgroups by being an observant spectator. While observing, take notes on the issues that could be raised during the analysis of the experience.

Unless the design requires, do not interfere—even if the rules are broken. When an activity does not seem to be progressing the way it should, it is helpful to remember that the learning comes from the learners' experience in completing the activity; the time to comment on what happened and how that might have affected their experience comes later, during the analysis and application.

Managing the Reporting Process

Depending on the nature of the activity and on your competence and preferences, the reporting process for a structured experience yields analyses and interpretations in varying degrees of depth and intensity. Typically the reporting process consists of three steps:

1. The trainer asks the learners to report what happened;
2. The trainer helps them to interpret what it meant; and
3. The learners make generalizations and develop applications to the real world.

A great many published structured experiences provide a list of questions for the trainer to use in helping learners to "process" the experience. Such questions suggest the general directions in which the analysis and application discussions may be led.

After the subgroups have completed their work, take an analytical stance in commenting about the way in which they worked and about the results they achieved. The "data" should be the focus of any comments; judgments about what the learners did during the activity should be avoided. Comments must be descriptive, not evaluative.

Avoid asking leading questions and forcing your preconceived conclusions or applications on the learners. Your job is to help the learners gain insight into their present behavior and how they might wish to change it. This means that you must know enough about the learners' real world to be able to help them derive relevant learning from the activity.

Role Plays

Role plays require learners to assume active roles in a simulated situation. For example, a common format calls for assembling the learners into subgroups of three. Within each subgroup one member assumes a particular role, such as that of supervisor or salesperson or interviewer; another member assumes the role of subordinate or customer or individual being interviewed; and the third member assumes the responsibilities of an observer. (A role play also can be a demonstration in which two or more people act out prescribed, detailed roles according to prescribed directions involving a very specific scenario, but we do not use the term "role play" in this sense.)

The usual purpose of role plays is to stimulate insight into behavior. A role-play activity frequently requires learners to employ their usual or typical behaviors in response to a given situation so that at the conclusion of the role play they can analyze their actions and resulting effectiveness. A role play also can be used to enable learners to experiment with behaviors that are potentially useful. "Reverse" role plays are those that allow learners to enter roles that are outside the realm of their usual experience; such role plays are commonly used to help learners to gain understanding of other people's viewpoints. They also work effectively when the objective is to see how others perceive particular individuals. For example, a supervisor might play the role of a subordinate; a reticent person might play an aggressive role; and a male employee might play a female employee.

A typical role-play design involves the following sequence of events:

1. The trainer introduces the role play and provides instructions.
2. The trainer explains the various roles.
3. Learners are assisted in becoming familiar and comfortable with their roles.
4. Role plays are conducted within subgroups.
5. The learners analyze their reactions to the role-play experience.
6. The learners draw generalizations and make applications to the real world.

Giving Task Instructions

As is the case with structured experiences, you must ensure that the introduction includes an explanation of the potential usefulness of the activity to the learners. If a rationale does not appear in the design, construct one, incorporate it into the introduction, and then check with the learners to ensure that they understand and accept it. Sufficient time should be allotted to provide clear, precise instructions and to determine that these instructions have served their purpose.

Part of the purpose of instructions is to prepare learners psychologically for the task so that they become familiar and comfortable with their roles before they begin the role play. Sometimes learners may simply be told to take a few minutes to read through the descriptions of their roles and to reflect on what behaviors might be appropriate to perform them. Sometimes, particularly for "staged" role plays, the design advises individual coaching on roles while those who are to be observers read and digest the observation guidelines.

It is important that you disclose all information that can be shared with the learners. If the design will not be damaged by telling everyone about all the roles, you should do so. Observers should be told what they are to look for during the course of the role play. In summary, you should offer as much information as the design permits; in this way a supportive climate is fostered instead of one that feels manipulative or risky.

Another suggestion for helping learners to become comfortable with a role play is to ask them to accept and adopt the facts of their roles. Explain that they are permitted to change their attitudes and behavior patterns during the action and to become emotionally involved, as long as they do not slip out of their roles. However, caution them against overacting because doing so may undermine the learning goals.

Finally, no one should be forced to participate in a role play, especially a staged one. Learners should be allowed to opt for an observer role or simply to watch unobtrusively.

Monitoring

In many role-play designs, one or more learners act as observers of the action, using a set of guidelines provided by the trainer. In addition, you must be an astute observer, moving from group to group when there are multiple role plays occurring simultaneously. Take notes on the action, concentrating on particular behaviors or issues that will be fruitful for analysis.

Remember that you are responsible for the learners' sense of security and safety as well as for facilitating their learning. This means that intervention is not only necessary but also appropriate when a role play becomes out of control or too intense.

Reporting

Helping the learners to come out of their roles is your first concern for effective processing. Before their attention is focused on what they learned, they should be allowed time to vent their feelings about what they have just experienced. Role plays can be emotionally charged experiences. Those learners who were most involved emotionally or who took the greatest risks should be given the first opportunity to express their reactions and feelings. Learners should be allowed as much time as they appear to require to come out of their roles fully. Once this has been accomplished, you can use the standard procedures— from Chapter 7 and from the previous section on structured experiences—to help the learners to make appropriate connections between their experiences during the role play and their own personal work situations.

INTERPERSONAL-SKILL-PRACTICE ACTIVITIES

Although they are similar in concept, interpersonal-skill-practice activities differ from role plays in that their major purpose is to allow the learners to develop and practice new skills. Skill-practice activities also assist people in gaining insight into the effectiveness of their current behavior. For example, a learner might practice conducting an interview with another learner who is instructed to act like a typical job applicant.

When preparing to manage skill-practice activities, review the pointers provided in the sections on subgroup-discussion activities and simulation activities. In addition, two other elements are critical to the success of these kinds of activities: realism in the practice, and performance feedback that is constructive.

Realistic Practice

When explaining the rationale for the activity, you need to emphasize to the learners that the skill practice is intended to closely approximate real situations that they have encountered or will encounter in the future. In introducing an interviewing skill practice, for example, stress that the learners will not be *playing* the role of interviewer, as in acting; instead, they will be *in* the role of interviewer. It is important to explain that the learners are expected to demonstrate the target skills, as realistically as possible, by responding appropriately to the situation. When monitoring a skill-practice activity, your main concern is to ensure that the learners respond realistically. If they do not, you must intervene and correct.

As is the case with role plays, you should check for charged emotions at the beginning of the reporting process and allow the learners to vent these emotions if necessary. Then you should focus directly on the behaviors demonstrated in the skill practice and how they will be applied or, if necessary, changed.

Giving Constructive Feedback

Without constructive feedback on their performance in a skill practice, learners have no way of knowing which behaviors they need to change, which they need to develop, and which they need to retain. The most important thing that you must do when using skill-practice methods is to give the learners accurate feedback on their performance—or carefully manage the process by which other observers provide feedback.

In order to be constructive, feedback must be descriptive rather than evaluative; it must focus on specific behavior, not general performance; and the learner must want it. Feedback in skill-practice situations is meant to do two things: to reinforce effective behaviors and to suggest improvements for next time. This prevents skill development from becoming a trial-and-error affair. Keep in mind that unwanted feedback usually produces very little behavior change. We have found that the best approach is to ask the learner who has just completed the skill practice to comment on his or her behavior first and then ask whether feedback from other learners and observers is desired. It never hurts to reiterate the ground rules for giving feedback each time the process is initiated.

NONVERBAL ACTIVITIES

Nonverbal activities are sometimes used when the learning goals for a program involve changes in attitudes, values, or interests. In management and sales training, reflective activities involving mental imagery or fantasies about the past, present, or future are now fairly common. They are often used to stimulate action planning: "Imagine yourself working here five years from now. Think of all the important things that you have accomplished. . . ." Sometimes nonverbal activities are used to help someone appreciate another's point of view: "Put yourself in your subordinate's position. How do you see. . . ?" The overall purpose usually is to stimulate reflection, understanding, or insight.

Most nonverbal activities are risky for the inexperienced trainer because learners tend to suspect that they are being "set up" or "psyched out." Activities involving imagery and guided fantasy, however, are an exception. If such an activity is straightforward and based on reality, it is relatively safe for even the inexperienced trainer and can add significant depth and meaning to learners' knowledge, understanding, and skill development.

It is essential that you feel comfortable and skillful enough to conduct an imagery or fantasy experience. You must feel sufficiently relaxed to be able to create an atmosphere for productive imagery. For a guided fantasy, you must be able to describe the physical and emotional surroundings of the fantasy situation in precise and colorful detail.

Before you introduce such an activity, make sure that the atmosphere in the room is conducive to introspection. For example, any audio and visual distractions should be eliminated, if possible. The introduction/rationale should be kept simple and brief. Be careful not to devalue the activity by labeling it "a little experiment" or "a fun thing to try." In addition, you should not contribute to learner anxiety by saying something like "Now we're going to take a mental trip to help you reveal your fantasies about the future." The learners should be told what, if anything, they are expected to report at the end of the experience.

At the beginning of the instructions, the learners should be told to close their eyes, breathe deeply, and relax as they imagine themselves in the situation to be described. Sometimes people are uncomfortable with silence. If there is nervous laughter, ignore it, stay comfortable and confident, and continue with the instructions.

The reporting process for an imagery or fantasy activity should be managed in a casual rather than demanding way. The significant learning has already happened, so you should not force or belabor the point. A few gentle probes are often sufficient: "What are your reactions?" or "Does anyone want to say anything?"

TEAM TRAINING

When two trainers work together to deliver a training design, there is great potential for synergy. Learners can benefit from being exposed to two trainer perspectives and styles, and each trainer can benefit from the added support. In most situations involving team training, it is helpful, but not critical, to have both trainers actually present in the room at the same time. In this way they can enhance each other's delivery by filling in gaps, providing illustrations or examples, and facilitating transitions from one segment to the next.

There are three main approaches to team training. Probably the most common approach is to divide a particular training program into distinct segments, with the two trainers assuming responsibility for different segments. For example, in a training session on managerial skills, one trainer may deliver a segment on communication and the other may deliver a segment on delegation.

A variation of this approach is to divide closely related segments between trainers. For example, one trainer might deliver a presentation on a particular subject, such as communication, and the other trainer might conduct an activity on the same subject. Although both trainers feel responsible for the entire program, one trainer takes a lead role and the other takes a backup role. In this case the transitions from one segment to the next are critical. Obviously, both trainers must be in the room at the same time.

With both of these approaches, the physical positioning of the trainer who is not facilitating at the moment (referred to here as the secondary trainer) is important. We suggest that the secondary trainer be either on the side or in the back of the room. It is not advisable for the secondary trainer to be seated or standing in front of the group. This position forces the secondary trainer into a situation in which he or she must constantly model attentiveness to the primary trainer at the expense of monitoring learner reactions. In addition, it can be intimidating to the primary trainer to feel that the secondary trainer is constantly watching every move.

A third alternative is a situation in which the two trainers are *equally* responsible for all or part of a training program. In this case both trainers remain in front of the group, although one may be slightly to one side while the other is talking. They frequently interact with each other as well as with the learners. When this kind of interaction is accomplished smoothly, the learners cannnot tell which trainer is the lead and which is the backup. Effectiveness in this approach requires practice, experience with each other, complementary (although not necessarily similar) styles, and healthy egos.

With all three approaches, the following tips may be helpful:

- Decide well in advance of the training session who is to do what and when.
- Work out signals that clearly communicate to the other trainer such information as "I have something to add," "It's time for a break," and "Pick up the pace."
- Agree on a plan to support each other if problems arise with the content and/or the group. This means working out a signal that communicates "I need help!"
- Decide on the "opening routine"; determine which trainer will serve in the primary role and which in the secondary role for each segment; and figure out how to handle disagreements, how to accommodate differences in style, and so forth.

- Use breaks as a chance to talk with each other for the purpose of critiquing, adjusting the design if necessary, renegotiating, changing approach or responsibilities, and so forth.
- If a lead and a backup trainer are involved, make certain that the backup trainer has some active role early in the program. It is important that the learners hear from both trainers before too much time has passed.

An important perspective to keep in mind when involved with a team-training program is that both trainers are models to the learners. If the learners witness collaboration, they will be more likely to collaborate in subgroup activities; similarly, if they see negative conflict between the two trainers, they may take fewer risks and demonstrate less openness.

Team training can be a joyful experience for both trainers as well as for the learners. Its effectiveness as an approach is tied to the trainer's choice of co-trainer, the amount of practice and preparation that both trainers devote to a good instructing relationship, and the mutuality of purpose demonstrated by the trainers during the training session.

Chapter 9

After the Session Is Over

After the session several matters may need your attention. For example, if someone has assisted during the training experience, you should express thanks to this person, exchange a few reactions, and perhaps make an appointment to meet later to share thoughts and feelings. In addition, you may need to straighten or clean the training room and store materials and supplies; if this is the case, using a check list is highly recommended. The most critical of your post-session responsibilities, however, is the review of learner evaluations and the analysis of your own feelings about how the session went.

EVALUATION FORMS

The last activity of most training programs is the learners' completion of some type of evaluation form. Such forms can provide you with valuable data on the learners' reactions to the program and their predictions regarding its usefulness on the job. Although the design of evaluation forms is not within the scope of this book, this chapter does deal with the use and interpretation of such forms. You should refer to the Resources appendix for references on designing evaluation forms.

Using Evaluation Forms

Always allow time within the session for completion of evaluations. If learners must stay after the session to complete their forms, they may do a perfunctory job and omit valuable information. Some people may want to complete their forms outside the session and return them later, but you should discourage this approach; it usually results in a low return and it delays the study of the results, adding to your administrative burden.

The purpose of evaluation forms is to seek learners' reactions. Therefore, evaluation forms should be distributed with as little fanfare as possible. We suggest that you employ the four-step process used in giving task instructions (see Figure 9-1).

"A great deal of information has been discussed, and you've had a chance to improve your skills. I hope you have found the program meaningful.

"Through your feedback about this program, you play a key role in improving future programs. In a moment you will have an opportunity to complete a prepared evaluation form. Be as candid and descriptive as you can. Signing your name to the form is optional.

"Spend the last ten minutes working on your own to complete the form that I'm going to distribute.

"When you have finished, leave your form in the center of your table."

Figure 9-1. Sample Instructions for Evaluation

Analyzing Completed Evaluations

Completed evaluation forms require interpretation to be useful. You should not accept learner reactions as "fact"; instead, these reactions are simply opinions that must be examined carefully and compared with your own reactions in order to put them in the proper context.

Use learners' evaluations only for the purpose of gaining understanding that can help in delivering future sessions more effec tively. It is important to remember that the learners' immediate reactions are very subjective and that they must be tempered by your own observations and judgment.

Reactions to a training session usually conform to a bell curve that is slightly skewed toward the positive. Given a group of fifteen people, the curve might look something like that shown in Figure 9-2, with two people reacting negatively, two very enthusiastically, and most of the rest leaning toward the positive side to a greater or lesser degree. In such a situation, if the learners rated the training on a scale of 1 to 10, the average would be 6 or 7. If you find that reactions to the session comform to this kind of curve, there is probably no reason for concern.

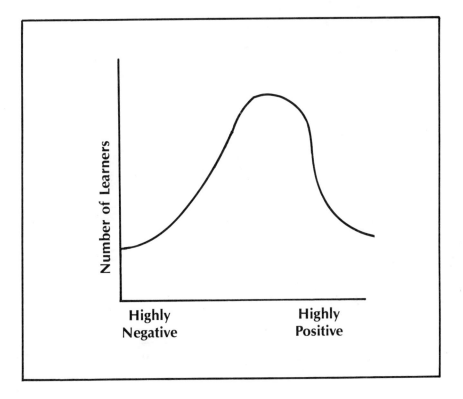

Figure 9-2. Typical Reactions to a Training Session

When the News Is Good

Sometimes evaluations are skewed as shown in Figure 9-3. When the evaluations are mostly very positive, you will probably feel quite elated. On many occasions highly positive evaluations accurately reflect a high-quality learning experience. Sometimes, however, overwhelmingly positive evaluations may result—at least, partially—from factors like the "halo effect," which creates deceptively positive ratings. Here is an example of how this effect might arise: A trainer ends a three-day training program by having each learner compliment every other learner. With the learners aglow with warm feelings, the trainer distributes the evaluation forms and instructs people to complete them. Although this concluding activity may be effective and appropriate, it will probably inaccurately skew the evaluation. Therefore, even when the responses are largely positive, you still should analyze them to make accurate judgments about what went well—and not so well—in the program.

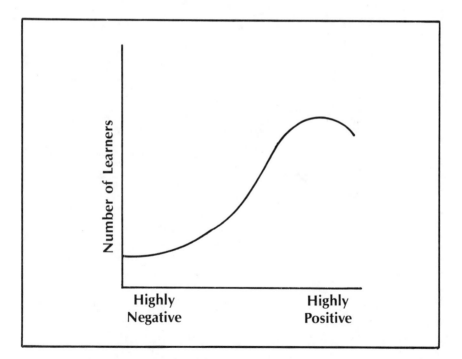

Figure 9-3. Learner Reactions Skewed in a Positive Direction

When the News Is Bad

Do not be devastated by a few extremely negative evaluations. One or two people in the room may be angry about being in the session, for one reason or another, and angry people sometimes evaluate inaccurately.

On the other hand, if the evaluations are more negative than positive, you must face the fact that something is wrong. The problem could be attributable to one or more of the following factors:

- *Inappropriate content.* The learners did not need the training or did not perceive a need for it.
- *Inappropriate timing for the session.* The learners needed the training, but they should have been doing something else at the time.
- *Outside factors.* For example, an upheaval in the organization may have interfered with people's learning.
- *Inappropriate selection of learners.* For example, the group may have been composed of people with drastically different levels of skill or knowledge.
- *Inappropriate design.* Simplistic activities, poor content organization, or the overuse of lecture may have seriously reduced the effectiveness of the program.
- *Inappropriate delivery.* It is possible that by dominating the learners, exhibiting weaknesses in delivery, preparing inadequately, or denigrating people, you may have interfered with learning.

If the evaluations are principally negative, you should analyze them to identify what factors, or combination of factors, led to the problem. It is important to consider the implications of a large proportion of unsatisfactory evaluations; discounting such responses is not helpful to one's growth as a trainer. Any problems can be corrected next time. It is also a good idea to remember that the learners' reactions are immediate ones and that they probably will change somewhat in the future. You may want to keep the evaluations and read them again just before the next session as a reminder of what to avoid.

DEALING WITH ONE'S OWN FEELINGS

You should recognize and pay attention to how you feel about the training experience. If the session went extremely well, celebrate and enjoy the emotional rewards of the experience. It is not recommended that you go back to work immediately. Instead, arrange to share your feelings with someone who will understand. This person could be your spouse, a friend, your supervisor, another trainer, or someone else in the organization.

On the other hand, it is equally important to recognize and to share your feelings if the training was a bad experience. When a training session is a disaster, it is usually impossible to be objective about it immediately; such an occurrence may cause you to feel miserable. We cannot recommend any instant remedies for such a feeling, but the following tips may be helpful:

Keep it in perspective. Everyone who has attempted training has conducted at least one bad session. With time, a more objective understanding of the experience will develop. The important thing to remember is that few failures have permanent effects if you learn from them. However, if serious problems persist, session after session, it may be advisable to seek some trainer-development opportunities. Some people ultimately decide that training is not for them, and those who make such a decision should congratulate themselves on developing enough self-awareness to come to this conclusion.

Experiencing anger over a failure is perfectly normal and understandable, but you should try not to dwell on the anger and should, instead, do something positive for yourself. Thoughts about past successes can be helpful, and so can the realization that anger passes and that self-confidence can be regained.

Take time to reflect. After assimilating your feelings about the training, take the time to examine the experience in terms of the parts that felt the most comfortable and the parts that generated the most anxiety. The reasons that some things went more smoothly than others should be determined. It is possible to use the skills that worked well in the successful parts of the training to improve performance in other areas that were troublesome. Data from the evaluations may help you to determine which skills to employ or to rely on more heavily in the future. Too often trainers are so busy planning for their next sessions that they omit this reflective step, but we believe that it is essential to one's development as a trainer.

CONTINUING LEARNING

In any well-conceived learning program, learning does not end when the formal session is over. Good programs encourage people to review and extend their learning to their work performance. The best programs not only encourage people to use their learning in the work place; they also offer a structured way of continuing learning and application.

The participant workbooks of many prepackaged programs include a mechanism for continued learning, coaching, and reinforcement. They typically encourage learners to engage in ongoing planning and suggest ways and offer opportunities for the learners to use the new concepts and skills on the job. They also encourage additional learning that might be required in the future.

Regardless of whether the program materials include such a workbook, you can do several things to promote continued learning:

- End the program by having learners brainstorm ways in which they plan to apply what they have learned.
- Ask learners to write a learning contract or action plan in which they specify what steps they plan to take, the resources required to take these steps, target dates on which the steps will be completed, ways to measure accomplishment, and so on. One approach is to instruct each learner to send a copy to his or her supervisor for follow-up.
- Phone or write the learners several weeks after the program to ask how they are applying what they learned.
- Send a follow-up evaluation form to learners three to four months after the session to elicit data on the application of learning as well as answers to other evaluation questions.
- Send each learner an article or news item related to the content of the program.

- Schedule a meeting with the learners' supervisors to discuss ways in which the supervisors can support and reinforce the new knowledge or skills gained in the training.
- Conduct a one-to-one follow-up consultation with each learner.
- Organize follow-up meetings, each of which is to be attended by some of the members of the original group. In each of these small meetings, the learners analyze their experiences in the work place, using the new abilities learned in the training session.
- Hold a follow-up training session.

We recommend that you plan related training sessions, particularly if management training is involved. It is important to identify other programs that will supplement, reinforce, and continue the learning process that has been initiated. Skill development, in particular, depends on continuing effort for mastery and transfer to the job.

Adults are people who have invested a lot of time and practice in being the way they are. Fostering behavior change all at once, through a single program, is virtually impossible. As learners test their new knowledge and skills in the work place, they are likely to feel some awkwardness and discomfort. One way for them to eliminate the discomfort is to discount or reject their new learning. Unless there is supportive follow-up to the training session, learners are quite likely to revert to their old behaviors, thus wasting much of the time and money invested in the training program. Although you do not have control over most of the variables that affect the learners' performance on the job, you do have a responsibility to encourage them to continue their learning.

Resources

We believe that the hallmark of a serious trainer is a continued interest in growth and learning within the training field. There are many resources available to help you to polish your skills and to develop other dimensions of training competence. Trainers often find membership in associations and networks particularly helpful; participation in the American Society for Training and Development, either through national membership or by joining a local chapter, is one example. Other groups can be identified by reading training journals and newsletters.

Another important way to continue your growth as a trainer is by attending trainer-training workshops and professional conferences, which provide many excellent opportunities for gaining knowledge of methods and media, for building skills, and for learning from the experience of other trainers. Professional training journals also can be an extremely useful medium for continuing learning. Some of these include *Training: The Magazine of Human Resources Development*, *Training and Development Journal*, *Training News*, *Data Training*, *Canadian Training Methods*, *Personnel Administrator*, *OD Practitioner*, and *Personnel Journal*.

In addition, there are hundreds of good books that can contribute to your growth. The following list includes some of the titles that we consider to be most useful in promoting trainer competence. These titles are organized according to whether their primary focus is learning philosophy, design and evaluation of training, or delivery of training. Books about delivering training that were written from a public-speaking or platform-skills perspective are not included in this listing. However, we have included relevant books written about delivery from an adult-learning (andragogical) point of view.

LEARNING PHILOSOPHY

Bell, C.R., & Nadler, L. (1985). *Clients and consultants.* Houston: Gulf.

Kidd, J.R. (1973). *How adults learn.* New York: Association Press.

Knowles, M.S. (1978). *The adult learner: A neglected species* (2nd ed.). Houston: Gulf.

Knowles, M.S. (1970). *The modern practice of adult education.* New York: Association Press.

Lippitt, G.L. (1973). *Visualizing change: Model building and the change process.* San Diego, CA: University Associates.

Nadler, L. (1979). *Developing human resources* (2nd ed.). San Diego, CA: Learning Concepts.

Rogers, C.R. (1969). *Freedom to learn.* Columbus, OH: Charles E. Merrill.

DESIGN AND EVALUATION OF TRAINING

American Society for Training and Development. (1976). *Training and development handbook* (2nd ed.). New York: McGraw-Hill.

Bell, C.R., & Margolis, F.H. (1982, August). Blending didactic and experiential learning methods. *Training and Development Journal.*

Bell, C.R., & Putman, A.O. (1979, May). Mastering the art of training design. *Training and Development Journal.*

Broadwell, M.M. (1970, October). The use and misuse of AV. *Training: The Magazine of Human Resources Development.*

Engel, H. (1973). *Handbook of creative learning exercises.* Houston: Gulf.

Knowles, M.S. (1975). *Self-directed learning.* New York: Association Press.

Laird, D. (1978). *Approaches to training and development.* Reading, MA: Addison-Wesley.

Lippitt, G., & Lippitt, R. (1978). *The consulting process in action.* San Diego, CA: University Associates.

Mager, R.F. (1975). *Preparing instructional objectives* (2nd ed.). Belmont, CA: Fearon.

Margolis, F.H. (1981, November). Discovery learning and technical material. *Training News.*

Margolis, F.H. (1970). *Training by objectives.* Cambridge, MA: McBer, 1970.

McLagan, P.A. (1978). *Helping others learn: Designing programs for adults.* Reading, MA: Addison-Wesley.

Nadler, L. (1982). *Designing training programs.* Reading, MA: Addison-Wesley, 1982.

Pfeiffer, J.W., Jones, J.E., & Goodstein, L.D. (Eds.). (1972, 1973, 1974, 1975, 1976, 1977, 1978, 1979, 1980, 1981, 1982, 1983, 1984, 1985, 1986,. . .). The *Annual* series for HRD practitioners. San Diego, CA: University Associates.

Pfeiffer, J.W., & Jones, J.E. (Eds.). (1969, 1970, 1971, 1973, 1975, 1977, 1979, 1981, 1983, 1985). *A handbook of structured experiences for human relations training* (Vols. I through X). San Diego, CA: University Associates.

Tough, A. (1972). *Adult learning projects.* Ontario: Institute for Studies in Education.

Weiss, C.H. (1972). *Evaluation research: Methods for assessing program effectiveness.* Englewood Cliffs, NJ: Prentice-Hall.

Zemke, R. (1982). *Figuring things out: A guide to task analysis.* Reading, MA: Addison-Wesley.

DELIVERY OF TRAINING

Bell, C.R. (1982). *Influencing: Marketing the ideas that matter.* San Diego, CA: Learning Concepts.

Bell, C.R., & Margolis, F.H. (1979). *A presenter's guide to conferences.* Madison, WI: American Society for Training and Development.

Cooper, S., & Heenan, C. (1980). *Preparing, designing, leading workshops: A humanistic approach.* Boston: CBI.

Davis, L.N. (1974). *Planning-conducting-evaluating workshops.* San Diego, CA: Learning Concepts.

Knowles, M.S., & Knowles, H.F. (1972). *Introduction to group dynamics.* New York: Association Press.

Margolis, F.H. (1979, March). Opening a conference with participative methods. *Training and Development Journal.*